Reaching Standards
Through
Cooperative Learning

Providing for ALL Learners in
General Education Classrooms

SCIENCE

Dr. Spencer Kagan

Miguel Kagan

Laurie Kagan

For information regarding this book and ordering other resources listed in the concluding section, contact:

National Professional Resources, Inc.
25 South Regent Street
Port Chester, NY 10573
1 (800) 453-7461
Fax: (914) 937-9327
www.NPRINC.com

For information regarding professional development, contact:
Kagan Publishing & Professional Development
1160 Calle Cordillera
San Clemente, CA 92673
(949) 369-6310
1 (800) WEE CO-OP
Fax: (949) 369-6311
www.KaganOnline.com

ISBN: 1-887943-37-4

Table of Contents

CONTENTS

Table of Structures & Activities

ACTIVITIES

This series is **dedicated to**

educators
sharing
the

VISION

of **ALL**

STUDENTS

reaching high academic standards

Acknowledgments

We would like to express our appreciation to all the people who made this video and Teacher's Guide series possible.

This project was initiated by **Dr. Robert Hanson,** President of National Professional Resources, Inc. It was Dr. Hanson's idea to create a series which would support the vision of helping all students reach high standards. Without the vision of Dr. Hanson and the support of **Angela Hanson** and **Andrea Cerone** of National Professional Resources, this series would not exist.

Dr. Darlene Schottle, Senior Director of Student Support Services for the Washoe County School District, provided the framework for adapting the structural approach to students with disabilities. Darlene provided input on how to adapt each of the Kagan cooperative learning structures for students with physical, cognitive, and behavioral and emotional disabilities.

Julie High, author of *Second Language Learning Through Cooperative Learning* and Director of Student and Family Services, North Monterey County Unified School District, provided the framework for adapting the structural approach to students whose primary or home language is not English. It was Julie's idea to adapt cooperative learning structures according to the stages of language acquisition. Julie provided adaptations for each of the structures in the series for students with various levels of English language fluency.

Jean Maddox, Principal, and **Diane Stepnitz**, special education teacher, Foster Road Elementary School, Norwalk-La Mirada Unified School District, La Mirada, California, generated activities using the structures to meet the math and language arts standards.

Laurie Kagan served as the video project coordinator. She was responsible for the selection of the structures and content featured as well as the training and coaching of teachers. Laurie co-directed with **Dr. Robert Hanson** the recording of classroom video. In addition to his authorship responsibilities, **Miguel Kagan** created and designed the layout of the manuals.

We are thankful to **Dr. Jim Hager**, Superintendent of Washoe County School District, who provided support for the project. We are especially thankful to the two principals from Washoe County Schools who graciously opened their schools to us: **Jackie Berrum**, Principal of Marvin Moss Elementary School in Sparks, Nevada, and **Trish Gerbo**, Principal of Hidden Valley Elementary School, Reno, Nevada. Jackie and Trish embody an ideal: Principals who are instructional leaders and who support and model inclusive and caring educational environments in which all students are supported in reaching the highest of standards.

Our appreciation extends to each of the following dedicated and talented teachers and trainers who allowed us to video them teaching with cooperative learning structures:

• **Denise Gordon** – 1st Grade: RallyTable for Math; Same-Different for Science; Blind Sequencing for Language Arts; and Line-Ups for Social Studies.

• **Laurie Kagan** – Coaching Teachers: Team-Pair-Solo for Math and Mix-N-Match for Science; 3rd Grade: Team Line Ups for Math; Find My Rule for Science; and Agree-Disagree Line-Ups for Social Studies.

• **Karen Karst-Hoskins** – 2nd Grade: Choral Practice and Turn Toss for Math; Songs for Two Voices and RoundTable for Science; Inside-Outside Circle for Language Arts; and Simultaneous RoundTable for Social Studies.

• **Lee Lin-Brande** – 3rd Grade: Formations for Math; Observe-Draw-RallyRobin for Science; RoundRobin for Language Arts; and Sequencing and Talking Chips for Social Studies.

• **Kathryn Pugh** – 5th Grade: Pairs Check for Math; Think-Pad Brainstorming for Language Arts; Timed Pair Share and Fan-N-Pick for Language Arts; Paraphrase Passport for Social Studies; and Team Mind Mapping for Science.

• **Sally Scott** – 1st Grade: Similarity Groups for Science; Team Interview for Social Studies; and Give One, Get One for Language Arts.

We are thankful to **La Vonne Taylo**r for her thorough and thoughtful job of copy editing.

And, of course, we extend our thanks to the hundreds of students who allowed us to video them as they used cooperative learning structures to reach the standards.

chapter
ONE

Reachining the Standards

As this series of videos and associated Teacher's Guides goes to production, there is a growing backlash in the country against the standards movement. And there should be.

Although there is great value in the standards documents themselves, there are serious problems with how the standards are being implemented and assessed. Some directions education is heading in the name of standards bode poorly for teachers, students, and our future. Paradoxically, the standards movement often impedes students' ability to reach the highest academic standards.

When standards become a mandate to make content knowledge the primary focus of education, a parade of negative consequences follows. When factual information becomes the driving force, we reduce our role as educators. We limit the development of our students. And we place our nation at risk. We are no longer engineers of meaningful learning experiences; we become transmitters of factual knowledge. Students are no longer unique gifts to be nurtured in their personal and academic development; they are empty vessels to be filled. And the role of education is no longer to prepare students for their future as happy and productive members of a democratic society; it is to hold teachers, schools, and districts accountable for scoring well on a standardized test.

Life is not black or white, right or wrong, or true or false. Nor should be the education of our nation's youth. Abhorrent and indefensible practices are springing up in the name of standards. Teachers are replacing valuable life lessons with quantifiable information that will translate into a right or wrong answer on the test. In some districts, rich schools are being given more money than poor schools because students in the rich schools are scoring better than those in poor schools on standardized tests!

Understandably, there is a backlash against standards. The problem is not that we have outlined rigorous academic standards. The problem is the way in which standards are being implemented and assessed. To equate the legitimate use of standards with the current standards movement, and to reject both, is to throw the baby out with the dirty bath water.

Content knowledge is necessary. It is helpful. Where would we be with a population of students who lack the content knowledge of the core disciplines? What would our nation be like if we were graduating high school seniors who couldn't read or write? How could anyone argue in favor of failing to provide a basic understanding of scientific knowledge? Failing to develop the ability to perform mathematical calculations? And in favor of producing uninformed citizens, who are simply unable to compete with their global peers?

Indeed, there is value in standards, but it is the implementation of standards that is crucial. The standards movement has focused on curriculum and assessment to the neglect of instruction. But it is focus on instruction which remains our best hope of having all students maximize their potential to reach the highest of academic standards.

This series of Teacher's Guides and videos is offered in an attempt to provide a model of how we can help all our students reach their potentials through effective instructional strategies. The model is the Kagan Structural Approach. This approach integrates cooperative learning, multiple intelligences, inclusion, and second language learning. It provides both the vision and the methods missing in much of the standards movement. Students not only achieve higher academic standards, but they rediscover the joy of learning in the process. They appreciate their classmates for their uniqueness. And they assume a new social orientation: Students are not motivated by a fear their competitor might know more or score better. They are motivated by engaging content and the meaningfulness of working and learning together.

Before previewing the Kagan Structural Approach, the basis for this Reaching the Standards series, let's briefly examine some problems we're facing with the current standards movement. This examination illustrates the importance of an approach to reaching the standards that sees beyond facts and testing. The Kagan approach provides a clear vision of how to nurture the development of essential skills in tandem with content knowledge. Adopting standards does not necessitate a return to an antiquated paradigm.

The new challenges we face entering the 21st century require a new approach.

Problems with the Standards Movement: Outcome Oriented, Not Process Oriented

All educators appreciate the importance of creating meaningful, engaging curricula. Paradoxically, the standards movement in its present form is causing teachers to create less meaningful and less engaging curricula. Part of the motivation for the creation of standards was the recognition that curriculum in many areas had become "an inch deep and a mile wide." Content area specialists who created the standards in each domain aimed to help teachers teach for depth, not breadth; to move away from teaching discrete, disassociated facts and toward teaching for meaning and understanding.

Unfortunately, the standards movement in its present form pushes teachers toward atomizing the curriculum, converting our classrooms into arenas in which our students win or lose in games of trivial pursuit. Instead of exploring mathematical relationships, students are memorizing math facts; instead of engaging in the scientific inquiry process, students are memorizing the findings of scientists; instead of engaging in historical reasoning, students spend their time memorizing facts for the history exam — facts soon to be forgotten. The focus on outcome, to the neglect of the process, is a gross violation of accumulated wisdom about teaching and learning. Learning which is not a by-product of genuine engagement is at best retained only for the test, never for a lifetime.

Behind the language arts standards is a clear desire to create among students a love for listening, speaking, reading, and writing. Paradoxically, the standards movement as it is being implemented creates among students a dread of language learning. Explicit in some of the standards benchmarks is the desire to generate among students an understanding of interdependence and the ability to work well with diversity; the standards movement, however, as it is playing out devalues diversity.

How has this paradox come about? How is it that farsighted and thoughtful standards have given birth to a shortsighted, self-defeating standards movement?

The problem is this: Once the standards visions were generated, benchmarks were created to outline the desired objectives for students at different levels. Given these benchmarks, well-intended educators created tests to determine the extent those benchmarks were being reached. Focus shifted away from the standards themselves and toward assessments that would show how well students were performing based on the standards. Various standardized tests were created, some much better than others. But all too often in the process of focusing on outcomes, focus on the meaning of the standards and ways to reach them has been lost.

Farsighted discussions of curricula were replaced with a shortsighted focus on test scores — scores on multiple choice, true-false, and short answer tests. This shift from curricula to assessment has had a number of negative consequences.

Narrow focus on scores on standardized tests creates pressure on teachers to "cover the curriculum" in a frantic attempt to increase test scores. In the process, teachers and administrators spend less time considering ways to teach for understanding and spend more time preparing students for tests, often tests which are strings of trivial, unrelated items. Whereas explicitly the standards value depth of thinking, implicitly the standards movement creates pressure toward superficial coverage of the curriculum. Paradoxically, the standards vision, born of an attempt to move beyond memorization of discrete, meaningless facts, has produced the very thing it intended to counter!

The parade of undesirable consequences of the present standards movement is long. See box: Problems with Present Standards Movement.

The Problems with Standardized Tests:
Evaluative not Informative

"Experience is the worst teacher, it gives the test before presenting the lesson." —Kimnesha Benns

Experience is really a wonderful teacher. It is through experiential lessons that we create meaning for our students. Our nomination for the "worst teacher" award is the standards movement's very own — standardized tests. The ways in which standardized tests are constructed and administered reveal they are not oriented toward improving teaching or raising academic excellence among students.

Problems with the Present Standards Movement

• •

• Increased pressure on teachers, associated with anxiety which in turn constricts teaching. Rather than exploring the teachable moment and modeling engagement with and enjoyment of the curriculum, teachers become more and more narrowly focused on "covering the curriculum" — whether or not they are building among students a love for and engagement with the content. If we believe the ancient adage, "The lesson that is not enjoyed is not learned," we must conclude that the present standards movement ensures that many lessons are not learned.

• Increased pressure on students, associated with increased anxiety and decreased liking for content, school, and education.

• Creation of standardized tests which dilute both curricula and instruction.

• Focus among teachers and students on test performance rather than on learning, outcomes over process, curriculum over instruction.

• Emphasis among teachers on breadth of coverage rather than depth of understanding, and quantity over quality.

• Valuing memorization of facts rather than acquisition of skills, and performance rather than engagement and understanding.

• Viewing students as containers into which the curriculum is to be poured, rather than as thinking, developing human beings.

• Ignoring individual differences in how students learn and how students best express what they have learned.

• Focus on absolute performance rather than on learning and improvement with a consequent devaluing of students with disabilities and those for whom English is a second language.

• Metacommunication to students that their worth is measured by standardized tests, rather than their learning and engagement with the curriculum at a developmentally appropriate level.

Why do we test students? In theory, we sacrifice valuable classroom time for testing only because it will inform the teacher and will improve teaching. Ideally, teachers would teach, assessment would be conducted, and teachers would then receive constructive feedback, support, and coaching. The goal of testing should be to teach the teacher how best to improve outcomes for students.

But the way standardized tests are administered, they are the worst teachers. If a test is given at the end of the school year, as a one-time event, there is little possibility for it to benefit the teacher or the students who have taken the test. The test then is rightly perceived by both students and teachers as part of an evaluation process, not part of a continual improvement process.

The way many standardized tests are constructed obviates their usefulness as informative instruments. Norm-referenced tests are constructed by selecting items which most discriminate among students. Let's take an example. Let's say it is very important for students to know item A and not very important at all for students to know item B. Let's say further that during test construction it is found that either almost all students or very few students can answer item A correctly. Item A is then found to be "non-discriminatory," and is tossed out. Further, let's say about half the students pass item B and half do not. Item B, then, is declared to be "highly discriminatory," and is retained.

Thus, in the construction of a norm-referenced test, it is quite possible for an item of little importance to be retained while an item of great importance is discarded. Discriminatory power, not importance, is what determines which items are retained and which are discarded in forming the final standardized norm-referenced test.

Let's take our example one step further. Teachers under pressure to have their students perform well on the standardized test are likely to emphasize item B (which is of little academic merit) and skip over item A (which is of great importance). Standardized tests clearly are not designed to improve curriculum or instruction; they are designed to discriminate and rank students. The way in which standardized tests are constructed and administered, reveals they are designed to rank students; the are not designed to improve instruction or raise excellence among students. Standardized tests are poor teachers: they fail to inform teachers how to teach better.

Even more contemptuous than the design of the tests is the content of the tests themselves. By far the most prevalent standardized tests are high-consensus tests with multiple choice or right or wrong answers. These tests make it easy to score and rank students on their mastery of factual knowledge. But by virtue of their very design they leave out skills that are equally, if not more, important than facts: thinking skills, technology skills, communication skills, personal skills, and social skills.

Brain research suggests inconsistencies, and uncertainties grow neuronal connections. The search for meaning is what makes us smart, not the memorization and regurgitation of facts. Our notion of what it means to be intelligent is broadening, and this expanded notion of "smart" is not captured by standardized tests. Students have multiple intelligences. Emotional intelligence is more predictive of life success than is IQ. Because some skills and educational objectives are not so easily quantifiable and don't translate well to standardized tests this surely does not mean that we as educators should not value them!

So we are faced with a dilemma. On one hand, we have standards and content knowledge which are of great value. Associated with the standards movement, but not necessarily the standards themselves, are pressures to stuff students with facts, teach to the test, and impose despised sanctions and incentives to pressure students into scoring well on standardized tests. On the other hand, we have important life skills and virtues we wish to nurture in our students. And a broader vision for the process of education. Which do we choose?

Fortunately, this is a decision we don't have to make. We can reach high academic standards in the process of developing successful life skills. In this series we illustrate how the Kagan Structural Approach is an effective approach for helping all students reach the standards.

The Kagan Structural Approach:
Reaching the Standards for ALL

The Kagan Approach is an interactive, inclusive approach to education based on some strong beliefs. We believe it is not only more desirable but also more effective to have students learn within inclusive, hetero-geneous classrooms. Research strongly supports the con-clusion that cooperative, inclusive classrooms promote greater academic and social gains. We believe that learning is a journey students each take to construct their own knowledge, not a race to master facts. And we believe that our ultimate mission as educators is to nurture students' development academically, socially, and emotionally, not just enable them to score high on standardized tests.

An Inclusive Approach

Classrooms are becoming increasingly heterogeneous and we are becoming more cognizant of the ways in which individuals are unique. Many of today's general education classrooms are quite diverse. Students who historically would have been members of special educa-tional programs are now being included in regular class-rooms. Inclusion legislation promotes the inclusion of students with disabilities in regular classrooms. Bilingual programs are being disbanded and the influx of second language learners in regular classrooms is increasing. Cultural diversity is increasing. Research on learning styles and multiple intelligences informs us just how diverse our classrooms really are — each student has a unique pattern of intelligences and unique styles of learning.

In theory, diversity is terrific. We appreciate and embrace the uniqueness of each learner. But how do we handle such diversity in practice? The approach presented in this series has proved to be successful for dealing with diversity. It is a unique synthesis of the work in cooperative learning, multiple intelligences, second language learning, and inclusion. The structural approach is based on the use of a wide range of simple instructional strategies, or structures.

Most of the structures presented in this series are based on heterogeneous cooperative student teams in the classroom. Students with disabilities and second lan-guage learners are included in teams with their peers. In the process of working and learning together through structured interactions, students with disabilities are truly included. Second language learners are exposed to a wealth of comprehensible input and highly contextual language, perhaps the single most important factor in language learning. Different structures engage different intelligences and appeal to different learning styles. Using a range of structures over time matches students' dominant learning styles and intelligences and provides a stretch for students to develop their nondominant intel-ligences.

It is in this cooperative, caring, inclusive, multiple intel-ligences environment that students can flourish academi-cally and reach their highest potentials. Educational theorists from different fields concur on the importance of cooperative, inclusive, safe classrooms. Brain research tells us that optimal learning occurs when there is challenge with the absence of perceived threat. Second language learning informs us that lowering the affective filter by minimizing anxiety and boosting self-esteem enhances language acquisition. And the literature on inclusion expounds the importance of establishing a classroom environment structured for successful inclusion.

An Integrated Approach

The Kagan Structural Approach is an integrated approach to teaching. It integrates the effective educational practices of cooperative learning, multiple intelligences, brain-compatible learning, second language learning, and inclusion. And it integrates essential life skills — thinking skills, communication skills, social skills — in the process of acquiring content knowledge and reaching the standards.

The structures are instructional strategies that teachers can integrate into almost any lesson at almost any point. Rather than designing separate cooperative learning lessons, multiple intelligences lessons, second language learning lessons, and inclusion experiences, the structures develop cooperation, engage students' multiple intelligences, and promote language learning and inclusion as part of every lesson. Rather than receiving separate lessons on the importance of inclusion, interdependence, and diversity, students experience the power of inclusion, interdependence, and diversity as a living reality in their daily work.

Rather than omitting essential skills in the rush to cover information on the test, skills are integrated into the process of working together. And these skills are arguably more important than the content. Consider the importance of these skills:

Thinking Skills

In the face of an accelerating information explosion, teaching one more fact is relatively useless compared to teaching how to think about facts. Whatever content we teach students today will be of relatively little use later in the 21st century compared to whatever thinking skills we can help our students acquire. Facts and theories can change. Thinking skills are skills for life. In the world of the 21st century, change will increase at an exponential rate as technological advances build on new scientific discoveries. In the process, more and more information will be generated. We cannot predict just what information our students will deal with, but we can predict they will need the skills to think about new information. Their jobs will change and change again at a rate we can only dimly imagine. The constant becomes not the information of today that we can drill into them, but the thinking skills they can develop and use for a lifetime. Education should not aim at teaching disassociated and meaningless math, history, and science facts, but rather should aim at providing environments in which students engage in mathematical, historical, and scientific reasoning.

Communication Skills

Most jobs today are in the information segment of the economy as we increasingly generate, analyze, store, reproduce, and communicate information. The information segment of the economy is the fastest growing. Ability to process and communicate information is a survival skill for the 21st century. Thus, it is incumbent on us as educators to help our students improve listening, speaking, reading, and writing skills.

Teamwork Skills

Increasing technological interdependence brings with it increasing social interdependence. No one person working alone invents and builds a computer. Teams create software and computer components. Teams coordinate their efforts with other teams. Interdependence in the workplace increases in proportion to technological advances. Employers today are crying out for schools to give students teamwork and communication skills, and as we move further and further into the 21st century, the call for teamwork skills will become ever louder.

Diversity Skills

Demographics are shifting and the global economy is upon us. Both factors combine to multiply the importance of diversity skills. In the workplaces of tomorrow, our students of today will work closely with others whose language, culture, values, and thinking styles will differ dramatically from their own. To fulfill our mission as educators for democracy, we must prepare our students with diversity skills.

Indeed, abilities to think critically and creatively, communicate effectively, and work with and respect others are crucial. As educators we need to prepare our students for the inevitable changes which will come with the 21st century. Our mission in schools is to prepare students well for the world in which they will live, a world in some respects quite different from our own. To help our students become successful, we must empower them with the highest thinking skills, communication skills, teamwork skills, and diversity skills. And many standards documents acknowledge the importance of these skills. They are explicit in many benchmarks and implicit in many more.

Mathematics

Student can explain to others how she or he went about solving a numerical problem.
Thinking skills, communication skills, teamwork skills.

Science

Student understands that questioning, response to criticism, and open communication are integral to the science process.
Thinking skills, teamwork skills, communication skills.

Social Studies
Student can describe how we depend upon workers with specialized jobs and the ways in which they contribute to the production and exchange of goods and services.
Thinking skills, teamwork skills, communication skills, diversity skills.

Language Arts
Student evaluates own and others' writing (e.g., identifies the best features of a piece of writing, determines how own writing achieves its purposes, asks for feedback, responds to classmates' writing).
Thinking skills, communication skills, teamwork skills, diversity skills.

The standards themselves are often visionary. Yet standardized testing is often short-sighted. Tests in their current form cannot easily measure the extent to which students work together successfully, respect others, appreciate diversity, and communicate effectively.

With the structures presented in this series, there is no need to discriminate between the facts and the skills. There is no need to focus exclusively on the facts that drive the accountability process. A curriculum of crucial life skills is embedded within each structure. Structures develop skills in the process of constructing content knowledge. It is hard to imagine achieving success with a range of standards without a range of structures.

Let's look at the structures we might use to reach these benchmarks. To reach the mathematics benchmark, we may use Team-Pair-Solo, a structure designed to move students from doing what they could previously do only with help to achieving independently. In Team-Pair-Solo, teammates share with their teammates how they solved the problem, be it a simple algorithm or building a concrete representation of a problem with manipulatives. Students acquire teamwork skills and communication skills in the process of developing their math content knowledge.

To reach the science benchmark, we may use Find My Rule to have students induce the rule for why things are being placed into different categories. Students develop their inductive reasoning skills, generate hypotheses, and communicate with teammates.

To reach the social studies benchmark, we may have students do a Team Interview. Teammates interview each other playing the role of someone with a with a specialized job. Students learn questioning skills, communication skills, and come to appreciate firsthand the unique contribution and specialized knowledge of each individual.

To reach the language arts benchmark, we may use the structure Give One, Get One. Students develop their writing skills, speaking skills, ability to work together, and appreciation of differing perspectives and styles as they take turns reading and evaluating a partner's writing.

The remarkable thing in each case is that embedded within the structure is the most important curriculum we can deliver. The Kagan Structural Approach is aligned with the lofty vision of fostering thinking, communication, teamwork, and diversity skills — all in the process of helping students reach high academic standards.

Looking Forward

Although we adamantly disagree with some of the directions in which education is headed in the name of the standards movement, we value the vision of reaching high academic standards. Further, we believe that the essence of the standards visions cannot be realized unless students interact cooperatively in diverse groups on a regular basis. Only then will students come to appreciate and celebrate the richness which results from the interaction created by diverse abilities, thinking styles, cultures, and languages. Only then will we truly be preparing our students for happy and successful lives in the 21st century. We provide this series as an invitation to try the Kagan Structures — to experience the satisfaction of seeing all students reach or surpass the standards.

Why Cooperative Learning & Science?

How

can we best structure learning so that our students will reach the highest standards in science?

The science standards are divided into four categories: Earth and Space Sciences, Life Sciences, Physical Sciences, and the Nature of Science. Within each category, students learn facts (the parts of a cell, the laws of motion) and acquire new ways of thinking. If we are successful in helping our students acquire a scientific orientation, they will think likes scientists for the rest of their lives. Generating and testing alternative hypotheses will be an ongoing process. They will think about their own behavior and the behavior of others in terms of the interdependence of all living creatures within an ecosystem.

How can we best structure learning so that students will acquire both knowledge and the habits of mind associated with the scientific inquiry process? We lean strongly in the direction of a process orientation. If we emphasize memorizing the content of science, students may learn facts, but they certainly will not acquire the thinking skills of a scientist. If, on the other hand, we emphasize process, or doing rather than memorizing science, students acquire both facts and thinking skills.

Emphasis on the habits of mind of the scientist is justified on a second ground: The information and technology explosion creates an ever-changing body of scientific content. Much of what we taught a few years ago is now outdated; much of the content we teach today will be outdated early in the 21st century. But the habits of mind, the process of science, will never be outdated.

When we give our students the gift of scientific thinking skills, we give them a gift for a lifetime.

How then, are we to structure so our students acquire knowledge about science in the process of obtaining scientific thinking skills? Teaching about thinking skills is not the same as having students acquire them. Having students memorize the steps of the scientific inquiry process is not the same as having them engage in that process so often that it becomes the way they think. Only if student engagement in the scientific thinking process is very frequent in the classroom will it become a habit of mind.

One solution is to structure the scientific thinking process into the instructional strategies we use on a daily basis. Many of the Kagan structures help us in this process. For example, in the video associated with this Teacher's Guide, we see students using Similarity Groups to sort and classify household items. We could substitute types of rocks, bones of the body, or celestial objects and still do Similarity Groups. The constant is that students are sorting and classifying. If sorting and classifying are to become a habit of mind, we want to use Similarity Groups often. And, wonderfully, in the context of that sorting and classifying, the students master any science content.

In the same way, we see students using a concept formation structure, Find My Rule, to induce the rule that distinguishes objects in each of two boxes — objects which sink and objects which float. Yes, the content is important; students need to know the types of things and the properties of things that sink or float. But at the same time, if Find My Rule is used, a scientific process is acquired: Students become more fluent in hypotheses generation and testing and inductive reasoning. But as with any of the Kagan structures, Find My Rule can be used with a wide range of content. Today, Find My Rule is used with objects which sink and float, tomorrow it may be used to discover a rule which distinguishes animate and inanimate objects, and next week it may be used again, this time to distinguish objects within our solar system and objects beyond. Only if Find My Rule is used repeatedly, with a range of content, will inductive reasoning become habitual for our students. If Same-Different is used repeatedly, students will acquire analytic skills as a habit of mind. If Observe-Draw-RallyRobin is used with a range of content, students will hone their observation skills, so central to much of science. The repeated use of the Kagan structures is a lifetime gift of scientific thinking skills. Over the process of their lifetimes, when our content is long outdated, they will continue to apply the habits of scientific thinking to content we now can only dimly imagine.

If we take the narrow road to having our students reach the standards, asking them to memorize the content of science, they will end up with neither the content nor the process. Memorization for a test is learning soon forgotten. Learning through cooperative hands-on, minds-on engagement is learning for a lifetime. The simple Kagan cooperative learning structures which are at the heart of this Teacher's Guide and series create the hands-on, minds-on engagement which allow both mastery of science content and acquisition of the scientific process.

What sticks, what endures for people are learning experiences based on engagement. Our students will reach the science standards to the extent that they are engaged in hands-on, minds-on learning experiences.

The memorization approach is a carry-over from the old factory model. Our students are empty, we run them through an assembly line of curriculum and classes, fill them up with facts and information, and send them on. Whereas the assembly line may work well for building cars, it is a poor model for fostering in our students a scientific thinking orientation. What sticks, what endures for people are learning experiences based on engagement. Our students will reach science standards only when our classrooms are full of wonder — places where students categorize, analyze, question, experiment, discard unsupported hypotheses, tentatively adopt hypotheses we fail to invalidate, and present data in many forms. Our classrooms are mirrors. Mirrors that reflect the future. The thinking process of our students in today's classrooms are but a reflection of the habits of mind they will apply for a lifetime.

The Science Standards

The

standards movement is currently in full swing. It has been a major driving force in education for over a decade. Before we explore how we can help all students in general education classrooms reach the standards, let's examine the standards in more detail. In this chapter, we will review the genesis of the modern standards, discuss the rationale for establishing and implementing standards, observe the state of the standards-based reform movement, and preview the science standards for grades K–8.

The Genesis of Modern Standards

The standards movement springs from two converging forces. One is political direction, support, and financial resources; the second is professional subject specialist organizations.

Political Support for Standards

A Nation at Risk, the famous report by the Commission on Excellence in Education published in 1983, is widely cited as the impetus for the present focus on standards. The report painted a dismal picture of the future of education in the United States, and thus our nation's future: "Our Nation is at risk. Our once unchallenged preeminence in commerce, industry, science, and technological innovations is being overtaken by competitors throughout the world." The report admonished that "the educational foundations of our society are presently being eroded by a rising tide of mediocrity that threatens our very future as a Nation of people."

Further, "We have, in effect, been committing an act of unthinking, unilateral educational disarmament." The report goes on to cite alarming data illustrating the shortcomings of our educational system. See box.

A Nation at Risk

• Compared with other industrialized nations, American students were last on seven out of 19 on academic tests, and never first or second.

• Millions of American adults and high-school-age students are considered functionally illiterate by the simplest measures of everyday reading, writing, and comprehension.

• Scholastic Aptitude Tests (SATs) demonstrate a virtually unbroken decline of scores from 1963 to 1980.

• There has been a decline of the number of students and the proportion of students demonstrating superior achievement on SATs.

• High school students lack "higher order" thinking skills. Forty percent cannot draw inferences from written material; only 20% can write a persuasive essay; and only 33% can solve multiple-step math problems.

• Science achievement scores have been steadily declining.

• High school achievement is lower than 26 years ago when Sputnik was launched.

Source: Commission on Excellence in Education, 1983

The report created an unprecedented sense of urgency in the reformation of the educational system. The widespread consensus was that the system was broken and needed to be fixed. This heightened interest and renewed dedication to our nation's education was the impetus for waves of educational reform, including standards-based reform. One of the Commission's main recommendations to reverse the "tide of mediocrity" was to focus on standards and expectations:

> We recommend that schools, colleges, and universities adopt more rigorous and measurable standards, and higher expectations for academic performance and student conduct, and that 4-year colleges and universities raise their requirements for admission. This will help students do their best educationally with challenging materials in an environment that supports learning and authentic accomplishment.

With education high on the national priority list at the end of the decade, President George Bush and all of the country's governors convened in Charlottesville, Virginia for what they called the "Education Summit." Their objective was to change the entire educational enterprise. To their credit, they realized that top-heavy reforms would more likely stifle innovation and stagnate achievement than improve the educational system. They endeavored to establish shared national goals that could be met at the local level by those closest to the process, recognizing that educators and parents are the ones most capable of effecting change.

Standards aim to reverse the rising tide of mediocrity.

The Education Summit laid the groundwork for the National Education Goals, an ambitious set of six broad goals to be achieved by the year 2000. The National Education Goals Panel (NEGP), an independent, bipartisan, intergovernmental panel, later described the Goals:

> The Goals span a lifetime of learning. They paint a picture of what is possible when children enter this world healthy, and when they start school – and leave it – ready to learn, with enquiring minds poised to shape and enrich our democracy, culture, and productivity. (National Education Goals Panel, September 1994.)

In addition to the NEGP, Congress established the National Council on Education Standards and Testing. These two groups were designed to address the issue of standards and assessment and to monitor and report on national and state progress.

In 1994, under the direction of President Clinton and with support from Democrats, Republicans, and most U.S. education and business groups, Congress passed Goals 2000: Educate America Act. This landmark act elevated the six original Goals into statute and added two new goals addressing: 1) parental involvement, and 2) teacher professional development. Political support for standards is most evident in two of the original Goals directed specifically toward academic achievement. See National Goals on the following page.

National Goals

- **Goal 3:** By the year 2000, American students will leave grades 4, 8, and 12 having demonstrated competency in challenging subject matter including English, mathematics, science, history, and geography; and every school in America will ensure that all students learn to use their minds well, so they may be prepared for responsible citizenship, further learning, and productive employment in our modern economy.

- **Goal 4:** By the year 2000, U.S. students will be first in the world in science and mathematics achievement.

Source: National Educational Goals Panel

As these goals clearly indicate, among our country's highest educational priorities is to enhance academic achievement, especially in science and mathematics. These goals, especially Goal 3, raise a very important question. How do we define "competency"? Subject specialists, to whom we now turn, provided frameworks for how we should define "competency."

Subject Specialist Organizations
Professional organizations that specialized in content matter played a seminal role in the development of standards. The National Council of Teachers of Mathematics (NCTM) developed consensus on what students should know and be able to do to demonstrate com-

petency. In 1989, the NCTM published *Curriculum and Evaluation Standards for School Mathematics*. The publication was a systematic effort to identify standards at three developmental grade levels: 1) Grades K–4, 2) Grades 5–8, and 3) Grades 9–12. This publication became widely recognized, raising national awareness of the goals of the standards movement and their ramifications. Today, it remains arguably the most widely accepted standards publication.

Other subject-area organizations soon followed the NCTM lead. Many used the NCTM's standards as a conceptual model for identifying their own content area standards. Standards were identified and continue to be identified in other subject areas, including:
- science
- language arts
- history
- social studies
- the arts
- civics, economics
- foreign language
- geography
- health
- physical education
- technology
- behavioral studies
- life skills

Standards-Based Reform

The establishment of the standards themselves, although an integral part of the standards-based reform movement, are just one component of the standards movement. The movement also heavily focuses on accountability. The basic underlying premises of the movement, simply stated, are: Our nation should have educational standards. To strive for educational excellence, we need to establish specific educational goals. But we need to do more than just create objectives; we need to ensure that the educational goals that we set forth are being met. The following quotation from the National Research Council clearly illustrates the link between standards and accountability:

> Standards-based reform includes content standards that specify what students should know and do to demonstrate proficiency, and assessments that provide the accountability mechanism for monitoring whether these expectations have been met and by whom. In addition, standards-based reforms assume that schools should be held publicly accountable for student performance. (McDonnell & McLaughlin, 1997, p.3)

As this excerpt indicates, a major component of the standards movement is "accountability mechanisms." The standards have almost become synonymous with testing and public accountability.

There are three components of the standards movement:
1. The Standards
2. Assessment of the Standards
3. Implementation of the Standards
Exploring these interrelated components is essential to understanding the current state of standards-based reform.

1. The Standards

The first component of the standards movement is the standards themselves. Metaphors are often used to describe standards. They have been called "targets to shoot for," "goals to meet," "destination points," and "constellations by which to navigate." Put simply, the standards are what students should know and be able to do to demonstrate proficiency at a certain grade level.

Kendall and Marzano (1997) summarize the current state of standards:

> Efforts continue in the development and implementation of standards. For most subject areas, there is one or more set of standards published by a nationally recognized group of subject-area experts.

Most subject areas such as math, social studies, language arts, and science have at least one set of standards by subject-area professional organizations such as the National Council of Teachers of Mathematics (NCTM), National Council for the Social Studies (NCSS), National Council for Teachers of English (NCTE), and National Science Teachers Association (NSTA). Some subjects have many standards publications from many organizations. There is not complete consensus among educators on what the standards should be. Springing from the various groups and standards publications are different, and sometimes even competing, views of what students need to learn in school.

A recent report indicated 48 states are now involved in establishing standards (American Federation of Teachers, 1996). Many schools and districts have their own publications of standards which often translate national and state standards into a more specific implementation approach. Standards are an ongoing process, continuing to evolve. They are revised and expanded. The standards are interpreted, modified, and implemented at many levels: national, state, district, school, and teacher.

John Kendall and Robert Marzano (1997) set out to create an internally consistent model of standards for groups wishing to "generate their own standards and benchmarks or, more commonly, to revise and augment the standards and benchmarks provided by their local state department of education." They consulted 116 standards documents in 14 different subject areas. They analyzed the standards publications and generated a massive compendium of standards and benchmarks for K–12 educators. It is the most consistent set of standards to date. The Kendall and Marzano Compendium represents a great step in the direction of "standardizing" the standards.

As they note, there were some difficulties "created by the variety of perspectives taken by various groups on the scope, purpose, and nature of standards" (Kendall and Marzano, 1997). Examining the problems they encountered in attempting to synthesize the standards provides insight to the existing standards. They faced five major problems:

1. Many standards documents - For many subject areas, there are multiple sources of standards documents.

2. Different definitions of standards - Many different groups have a different definition of exactly what standards are, and some groups even use standards differently. Kendall and Marzano (1997) make an interesting distinction between two different types of standards they found when analyzing many standards documents. They distinguish between *content standards* and *curriculum standards*. Content standards focus on specific knowledge or skills that students should attain. Content standards can also be thought of as content knowledge. It is specific information relating to the subject area. Curriculum standards, on the other hand, focus on the goal of the subject matter, or how the curriculum should be presented to achieve a desired learning outcome. They argue that curriculum goals and principles should not be included in the description of content standards.

Content vs. Curriculum Standards

• **Content Standards -** Specific knowledge and skills for students to acquire.

• **Curriculum Standards -** Overarching goals or principles of subject area.

Source: Kendall and Marzano, 1997

3. Varying types of standards descriptions - The descriptions of the standards vary from document to document, and often within a document. Some standards are described as a procedural statement (what the learner is able to do); some standards are described as a declarative statement (what the learner understands); and some standards are described contextually (what the student is able to do when).

4. Different grade ranges - Different organizations and publications establish benchmarks for different grade levels.

5. Different levels of generality - Some standards are very specific; others are very broad in scope.

In examining Kendall and Marzano's efforts to reconcile the many and varied efforts to establish standards and benchmarks, it becomes obvious that although there is not complete consensus on the standards, the development of the standards is well underway.

2. Assessment

The second component of the standards movement is assessment. Multiple levels of accountability have been established through assessment. This accountability mechanism is designed to inform educators and the general public how well schools are doing at reaching the standards. A recent study on educational accountability systems found that 46 states administered statewide student assessments in the 1995–96 school year (Bond et al., 1996). With increased attention to assessments, nearly all states are now administering statewide assessments. Most states administer assessments in grades 4, 8, and 11. At least two states administer assessments in every grade from K–12. Assessments most frequently cover mathematics, language arts, and writing. Science and social studies are close behind. The most commonly used tests are writing assessments and criterion-referenced tests. Norm-referenced tests are frequently used, and performance assessments are seldom used. Only four states currently use portfolios as part of their statewide assessment. There is currently a great deal of activity related to statewide assessments; their characteristics are changing frequently (20th Annual Report to Congress).

Incentives and sanctions have been linked to the accountability systems and have become a recent area of focus in the standards movement. Schools and districts have been using sanctions (such as probational status) and rewards (such as teacher incentives) to promote academic achievement. By recent count, 30 states imposed consequences to students such as promotion, awards, and graduation; and 27 states applied consequences to schools such as awards to staff and loss of funding based on student performance (Bond, Braskamp, & Roeber, 1996; National Educational Goals Panel, 1996).

3. Implementation

The third component of the standards movement is implementation. Here, the main emphasis is on effective classroom practices that help students meet the standards. Implementing the standards is a challenge, especially when we adopt the noble goal of ALL students reaching the standards. Teachers are faced with increasingly diverse student populations. Increasing racial diversity is leading to greater heterogeneity within classrooms, especially in urban centers. As a consequence of recent inclusion legislation, students with disabilities who might in the past have been pulled out of regular classrooms and placed in special education programs are now being included in general education classes. Largely due to our nation's shifting demographics, but also due to disbanding bilingual programs, there are increasing numbers of students with limited English proficiency in "normal" classes. Theory and research on styles and multiple intelligences inform us that students have very different minds and learn very differently. With so many learners and so many different learners, the challenge becomes: How do ALL students reach the standards?

In this Teacher's Guide and the accompanying video series, we focus on how cooperative learning can be used as an effective teaching and learning vehicle for helping all students reach the standards. Research on cooperative learning finds strong positive outcomes in academic achievement. In the following chapter, we will explore the key concepts of effective cooperative learning, and in Chapter 8 we will look at specific practical applications that are used to successfully reach the science standards. The implementation of cooperative learning, by virtue of its inclusive design and multimodal structures, provides a very promising approach to reaching high academic standards with very diverse classroom populations.

The Rationale for Standards

Many cases have been made for standards. The National Educational Goals Panel describes the importance of standards: "Without standards to guide changes and link reforms, our initiatives are set to sail like a ship without a rudder" (NEGP, 1994). Dianne

Ravitch, author of *National Standards in American Education: A Citizens Guide*, is a chief proponent of the modern standards movement. She explains the importance of standards:

> Americans…expect strict standards to govern construction of buildings, bridges, highways, and tunnels; shoddy work would put lives at risk. They expect stringent standards to protect their drinking water, the food they eat, and the air they breathe.
> …Standards are created because they improve the activity of life. (Ravitch, 1995)

Some of the most compelling arguments for standards are that they: clarify expectations, enhance accountability, raise expectations and motivation, and equalize educational outcomes.

Standards Clarify Expectations

Identifying what students are expected to learn and what type of performance is expected in order to demonstrate proficiency provides a common direction for educators. Defining the standards for each subject and at each grade level quantifies the teaching and learning objectives. Districts, schools, teachers, and students have a clear mandate of what is expected of them. The first step to achieving success is setting goals. Standards set unambiguous educational goals.

Standards Enhance Accountability

Establishing a clear set of standards also enables accountability mechanisms to be employed. The argument is that holding schools, teachers, and students accountable for performance increases academic achievement. Again, educational research is consistent with this perspective: Accountability increases the likelihood of success. However, how accountability is being used and for what is currently in contention.

Standards Raise Expectations and Motivation

By clarifying expectations and accountability, expectations and motivation are raised. Districts, schools, and individual teachers have clear goals to aim for and will know whether or not their students are meeting the standards. When standards are not met, alternative approaches to curriculum and instruction are implemented. By creating standards, we increase the rigor and raise the level of performance. Standards raise expectations which in themselves may raise achievement. The argument goes something like this: If we set high standards for our students and teachers, and expect them to reach those high standards, they will. Much research on educational expectations support this basic premise.

Standards Equalize Outcomes

Perhaps the strongest philosophical rationale for adopting standards is the argument that standards equalize educational opportunity. One of the most basic tenents of education in our democratic society is that all students should have equal access to an equal education. At the national level, standards provide a uniform set of directives for teachers. Thus the standards apply pressure to equalize student outcomes. Regardless of race, ability, or socioeconomic status, what students are supposed to learn is the same across the board.

The Science Standards
Primary Reports on the Science Standards

- National Science Education Standards (National Research Council, 1994)
- Benchmarks for Science Literacy (Project 2061, 1993)
- Scope, Sequence, and Coordination of Secondary School Science: The Content Core (NSTA, 1993)

Professional Science Organization

National Science Education Standards
2101 Constitution Ave., NW
HA 486
Washington, DC 20418
(202) 334-1399

Overview of Science Standards

Earth & Space Sciences

1. Student knows the basic features of Earth.
2. Student understands the basic processes of Earth.
3. Student comprehends Earth's place in the universe and the essential composition and structure of the universe.

Life Sciences

4. Student understands the unity and diversity of life.
5. Student comprehends the basics of genetics.
6. Student knows the structure and function of cells.
7. Student understands the interdependence of species and the environment.
8. Student understands the role of matter and energy in the environment.
9. Student comprehends the basics of the evolution of species.

Physical Sciences

10. Student understands the basic properties of matter.
11. Student comprehends the types, sources, and conversions of energy and their relationship to heat and temperature.
12. Student comprehends the principles of motion.
13. Student understands the forces between objects and within atoms.

Nature of Science

14. Student comprehends the nature of scientific knowledge.
15. Student comprehends the nature of scientific inquiry.
16. Student comprehends the scientific enterprise.

Science Standards

The standards are presented with specific content knowledge for each of three grade ranges (K–2, 3–5, 6–8). For a more comprehensive presentation of standards, see Kendall and Marzano's book, *Content Knowledge* (1997). Their Compendium of standards may be accessed on the Internet: http://www.mcrel.org/standards-benchmarks/

Science Standards • Grades K–2

Earth & Space Sciences

1. Student knows the basic features of Earth.
- Student knows Earth is composed of rocks, soils, water, and atmospheric gases.
- Student knows water can change from a liquid to a solid (frozen) state and back, yet the amount of water remains unchanged.
- Student understands the weather may change daily and the weather patterns change with the seasons.

2. Student understands the basic processes of Earth.
- Student knows rocks come in many sizes and shapes (rocks, pebbles, boulders, sand).

3. Student comprehends Earth's place in the universe and the essential composition and structure of the universe.
- Student knows that the universe consists of a tremendous number of stars, of unequal brightness and unevenly dispersed.
- Student comprehends the basic characteristics of the sun (rises and sets daily; moves from east to west across the sky) and the moon (appears at night, but also sometimes in the day; appears to change shapes during the month; moves from east to west across the sky).

Life Sciences

4. Student understands the unity and diversity of life.
- Student understands that plants and animals have characteristics to help them survive in different environments.

5. Student comprehends the basics of genetics.
- Student understands plants and animals closely resemble their parents due to transfer of biological information.
- Student understands the uniqueness of plants (difference between two rosebushes) and animals (difference between two elephants) of the same kind.

Science Standards • Grades K–2 continued

6. Student knows the structure and function of cells.
- Student comprehends that animals breathe air, drink water, eat food, and require shelter.
- Student comprehends that plants require air, water, light, and nutrients.

7. Student understands the interdependence of species and the environment.
- Student knows that living organisms are found almost everywhere on Earth, and that different environments support different types of plants and animals.

8. Student understands the role of matter and energy in the environment.
- Student understands that plants and animals require energy in the form of food, water, and light.

9. Student comprehends the basics of the evolution of species.
- Student comprehends that some plants and animals have become extinct.

Physical Sciences
10. Student understands the basic properties of matter.
- Student understands different objects are made of different materials (metal, wood, plastic, fabric) and materials have different observable characteristics (color, shape, weight, size).
- Student understands things can be done to materials to change their properties (dissolving, mixing, heating, freezing) and different materials respond differently.

11. Student comprehends the types, sources, and conversions of energy and their relationship to heat and temperature.
- Student understands that the sun provides light and heat to Earth.
- Student understands heat can be generated in a variety of ways (burning, rubbing, mixing substances).
- Student knows that electricity can produce light, sound, heat, and magnetic effects.

Science Standards

Science Standards • Grades K–2 continued

12. Student comprehends the principles of motion.
- Student understands sound is produced by vibrating objects.
- Student understands light travels in a straight line.
- Student knows that pushing and pulling can change the position and motion of an object.

13. Student understands the forces between objects and within atoms.
- Student understands magnets can be used to move some objects without touching them.
- Student understands that objects near the earth fall down unless they are held up.

Nature of Science

14. Student comprehends the nature of scientific knowledge.
- Student comprehends scientific investigations are conducted similarly in different locations and some results can generally be duplicated.

15. Student comprehends the nature of scientific inquiry.
- Student knows that inquiry in the form of observations and experiments can produce learning.

16. Student comprehends the scientific enterprise.
- Student knows that in science it is helpful to work with a team and share findings with others.

Science Standards

Science Standards • Grades 3–5

Earth & Space Sciences

1. Student knows the basic features of Earth.
- Student understands differences between fresh and salt water.
- Student understands the states of water (solid, liquid, gas) and the processes involved (evaporation, freezing, boiling, condensation, precipitation).
- Student understands night and day is caused by Earth's rotation on its axis.

2. Student understands the basic processes of Earth.
- Student understands fossils provide information about plants and animals that lived long ago.
- Student understands how Earth's surface is in a constant state of change (via erosion, volcanic eruptions, earthquakes, landslides).
- Student understands the composition of rock and soil.

3. Student comprehends Earth's place in the universe and the essential composition and structure of the universe.
- Student knows several planets, including Earth, orbit the sun and the moon orbits Earth.
- Student knows that stars and planets are massive in size and are separated by vast distances.
- Student knows that stars move in patterns across the sky every night, and different stars are visible in different seasons.

Life Sciences

4. Student understands the unity and diversity of life.
- Student understands plants and animals progress through cycles of birth, development, reproduction, and death and that life cycles vary for different organisms.
- Student understands plants and animals may be classified in different systems and understands the basis for classification (plants/animals, pets/nonpets).

5. Student comprehends the basics of genetics.
- Student understands that many traits (eye color, mannerisms, color of flower) are inherited from the parents.

Science Standards

Science Standards • Grades 3–5 continued

6. Student knows the structure and function of cells.
- Student understands that organisms have different structures that are used for different purposes (eyes for seeing, mouth for eating, ears for hearing).

7. Student understands the interdependence of species and the environment.
- Student understands that behavior of organisms is influenced by internal (internal states) and external cues (environment, interactions).
- Student understands that organisms have an effect on their environment, some positive, some negative.
- Student understands that the changing environmental conditions effects different organisms differently.

8. Student understands the role of matter and energy in the environment.
- Student knows that energy (through food) is essential to all living organisms.
- Student knows the basic organization of food chains and food webs.

9. Student comprehends the basics of the evolution of species.
- Student understands that fossils can be used to determine information about past life.

Physical Sciences
10. Student understands the basic properties of matter.
- Student understands that materials may be composed of parts too small to be viewed with the naked eye.
- Student knows that materials have different states (solid, liquid, gas) and some materials can be changed from state to state by heating or cooling.
- Student knows objects can be classified according to their characteristics (density, conductivity, magnetism).

Science Standards

Science Standards • Grades 3–5 continued

11. Student comprehends the types, sources, and conversions of energy and their relationship to heat and temperature.

- Student knows that heat is often produced when one form of energy is converted into another form.
- Student knows the organization of a basic electrical circuit.
- Student knows that heat can move from object to object via conduction and that some materials conduct better than others.

12. Student comprehends the principles of motion.

- Student knows that when force is applied to an object, the object either speeds up, slows down, or changes directions.
- Student understands that a sound's pitch depends on the frequency of the vibration producing the sound.
- Student knows that light can be reflected, refracted, or absorbed.

13. Student understands the forces between objects and within atoms.

- Student understands that magnets attract and repel other magnets and other materials.
- Student understands that electrically charged material pulls on other materials and can either attract or repel other charged materials.
- Student understands that Earth's gravity pulls objects toward Earth.

Nature of Science

14. Student comprehends the nature of scientific knowledge.

- Student knows that repeated scientific investigations should yield similar results when conducted by different people, in different times, and in different places.

Science Standards

Science Standards • Grades 3–5 *continued*

15. Student comprehends the nature of scientific inquiry.

- Student understands that inquiry involves conducting investigations and comparing results to current knowledge.
- Student understands scientists use different types of investigations (observations, experiments) depending on the nature of the question they're trying to answer.
- Student conducts simple investigations including observations and experiments.

16. Student comprehends the scientific enterprise.

- Student understands individuals of all ages, cultures, and backgrounds have made contributions to scientific knowledge.
- Student understands that science is an unending process to uncover the mysteries of the universe.
- Student understands scientists often work in teams.

Science Standards

Science Standards • Grades 6–8

Earth & Space Sciences

1. Student knows the basic features of Earth.

- Student understands Earth is the only body in our solar system that supports living organisms.
- Student knows that Earth is composed of multiple layers (core, mantle, lithoshpere, hydrosphere, atmosphere).
- Student understands the processes of the water cycle (evaporation, condensation, precipitation, percolation) and their effects on climate.

2. Student understands the basic processes of Earth.

- Student understands that Earth's crust is divided into plates that move slowly in response to the movements in the mantle.
- Student understands land forms are created through constructive and destructive forces.
- Student knows that different types of rocks (sedimentary, igneous, and metamorphic) contain evidence of the minerals, temperatures, and forces that created them.

3. Student comprehends Earth's place in the universe and the essential composition and structure of the universe.

- Student knows that the universe consists of many billions of galaxies each with many billions of stars and that the distances between galaxies and stars is tremendous.
- Student understands gravity keeps planets in orbit around the sun and gravity keeps moons in orbit around planets.
- Student knows the characteristics of the nine planets in our solar system (size, order, moons, rings, composition).

Science Standards

Science Standards • Grades 6–8 continued

Life Sciences

4. Student understands the unity and diversity of life.
- Student understands the ways in which living organisms can be classified.
- Student understands that unity exists among organisms (as evidenced by similar internal structures, chemical processes, common ancestry) despite the variation in appearances.
- Student understands that there exists a great diversity of body plans and internal structures among plants and animals.

5. Student comprehends the basics of genetics.
- Student knows that reproduction is common to all living organisms and is essential for the continuation of a species.
- Student understands the differences between sexual and asexual reproduction, and the advantages and disadvantages of each.
- Student knows hereditary information is inherited though the genes.

6. Student knows the structure and function of cells.
- Student knows cells are the fundamental unit of life and that all organisms are composed of cells.
- Student knows that multicellular organisms have cells, tissues, organs, and organ systems that are highly specialized and perform specialized functions (digestive system, circulatory system, reproductive system).
- Student understands that energy in the form of food is used for cellular functions (growth and division, production and maintenance).

7. Student understands the interdependence of species and the environment.
- Student understands relationships exist among organisms in food chains and webs.
- Student knows organisms may regulate internal states enabling them to survive in a constantly changing environment.
- Student understands factors that influence the number and types of organisms that may be supported in an ecosystem (resources, competition, light, water, disease).

Science Standards • Grades 6–8 continued

8. Student understands the role of matter and energy in the environment.
- Student understands that energy is generated by the sun and is transferred from interdependent organisms in a food web.
- Student knows matter is recycled within ecosystems, is repeatedly transferred from organisms, and remains constant regardless of form and location.

9. Student comprehends the basics of the evolution of species.
- Student understands the basics of biological evolution.
- Student knows that fossil evidence documents the evolutionary history (appearance, diversification, and extinction) of many life forms.
- Student understands the concept of extinction and its ramifications for biological evolution (most species that have lived no longer exist; species incapable of adapting to Earth's changing environment become extinct).

Physical Sciences
10. Student understands the basic properties of matter.
- Student knows that matter consists of atoms, and different arrangements of atoms compose all matter.
- Student knows that atoms are in constant, random motion and the characteristics of atoms in different states (atoms in solids are close together and don't move about easily; atoms in liquids are close together, stick to one another, and move about easily; atoms in gas are far apart and move about freely).
- Student knows that pure elements are substances which contain only one kind of atom; there are over 100 kinds of elements; and elements may be grouped according to their characteristics.

11. Student comprehends the types, sources, and conversions of energy and their relationship to heat and temperature.
- Student knows that energy cannot be created or destroyed, only changed from one form to another.
- Student knows heat can be transferred by conduction, convection, and radiation; and that heat flows from warmer objects to cooler objects until both reach the same temperature.
- Student knows that electrical circuits can be used to transfer energy into sound, light, heat, motion.

Science Standards • Grades 6–8 continued

12. Student comprehends the principles of motion.

- Student knows that an object will continue to move at a constant speed and in a straight line unless it is subjected to a force.
- Student knows an object's motion can be represented graphically in terms of its speed, direction of motion, position.
- Student knows that differences in wavelengths of visible light are perceived as different colors; the other range of wavelengths cannot be detected by the human eye.

13. Student understands the forces between objects and within atoms.

- Student knows that magnets can cause electric currents and vice versa.
- Student comprehends general concepts relating to gravitational forces (every object exerts a gravitational force on every other object; gravitational force depends on the mass of the objects and their distance; gravitational force is difficult to detect in objects with little mass).

Nature of Science

14. Student comprehends the nature of scientific knowledge.

- Student knows that an experiment must be repeated many times and produce similar results before the results are accepted as correct.
- Student understands that many core scientific theories are confirmed by experimentation and observation, yet many are subject to change and improvement with future experimentation and observation.
- Student understands that questioning, response to criticism, and open communication are fundamental to scientific knowledge.

Science Standards • Grades 6–8 continued

15. Student comprehends the nature of scientific inquiry.
- Student understands that the "scientific method" is not a fixed procedure, but rather a process of investigation: developing a hypothesis, collecting data, and logical reasoning.
- Student knows how to design and conduct a scientific investigation.
- Student understands that observations can be influenced by bias.

16. Student comprehends the scientific enterprise.
- Student understands that the scientific field is composed of a great diversity of people who sometimes work together, sometimes work alone, but all communicate extensively with others.
- Student understands that the enterprise of science requires a great diversity of human skills.
- Student understands the associated ethical implications of scientific investigation.

SCIENCE Reaching the Standards Through Cooperative Learning
Kagan, Kagan & Kagan

Resources

• •

American Federation of Teachers. *Making Standards Matter 1996: An Annual Fifty-State Report on Efforts to Raise Academic Standards.* Washington, DC: Author, 1996.

Bond, L. A., D. Braskamp, & E. Roeber. *The status report of the assessment programs in the United States.* Oak Brook, IL: North Central Regional Educational Laboratory and Council of Chief State School Officers, 1996.

Bond, L. A., E. Roeber, & D. Braskamp. *Trends in state student assessment programs.* Washington, DC: Council of Chief State School Officers, 1996.

Kendall, John S., & Robert J. Marzano. *Content Knowledge. A Compendium of Standards and Benchmarks for K–12 Education, 2nd Edition.* Aurora, CO: Mid-continent Regional Educational Laboratory, Inc. and Alexandria, VA: Association for Supervision and Curriculum Development, 1997.

McDonnell, L. M., & M. J. McLaughlin. *Profile of State Assessment Systems and Reported Results.* Washington, DC: National Academy Press, 1997.

National Commission on Excellence in Education. *A Nation At Risk: The imperative for educational reform.* Washington, DC: Government Printing Office, 1983.

National Council of Teachers of Mathematics. *Curriculum and Evaluation Standards for School Mathematics.* Reston, VA: 1989.

National Education Goals Panel. *The National Education Goals Report: Building a Nation of Learners.* Washington, DC, 1994.

National Education Goals Panel. *The National Education Goals Report: Building a Nation of Learners.* Washington, DC, 1996.

Ravitch, Diane. *National Standards in American Education: A Citizens Guide.* Washington, DC: Brookings Institution, 1995.

U.S. Department of Education. *To Assure the Free Appropriate Public Education of all Children with Disabilities. Twentieth Annual Report to Congress on the Implementation of the Individuals with Disabilities Act.* Washington, DC: U.S. Department of Education, 1998.

Reaching the Standards Through

Cooperative Learning

Cooperative

learning has been around for a long time. It is perhaps the most extensively studied educational innovation of all time. Studies have consistently found cooperative learning outperforms individualistic and competitive classroom structures on a number of outcome variables, including academic achievement (Kagan, 1985). These findings establish cooperative learning as a prime candidate for reaching rigorous academic standards.

Hundreds of controlled research studies have established cooperative learning as one of the most powerful tools for producing academic achievement gains (Johnson, D. W., Maruyama, G., Johnson, R., Nelson, D. & Skon, L., 1981). One of the most remarkable aspects of this research is its robustness. Cooperative learning has consistent positive effects on achievement among primary, elementary, middle school, and high school students. The achievement gains hold up across the full range of academic content areas. And they are consistent across student populations, including urban-rural; lower-middle-upper income; and regular education-special education populations. The effects have been tested worldwide. There is no more robust set of findings in education. Thus, as we increasingly focus on meeting high academic standards, it is natural to turn to an approach with a proven track record of boosting academic outcomes.

Noteworthy are the types of gains promoted by cooperative learning. Students in cooperative settings not only outperform their counterparts in measures of academic achievement, but the gains are greatest for the lowest-achieving students (Kagan, 1985). These findings run contrary to the notion that achievement gains for the lowest achievers in cooperative learning is bought at the expense of the highest achievers. This empirical support is especially optimistic when faced with the challenge of an increasingly diverse student population. Cooperative learning provides a promising approach to reaching high academic standards.

In this chapter, we overview the Kagan approach to cooperative learning, called Kagan Cooperative Learning or the Structural Approach. We explore the six key components of creating an effective cooperative learning environment in which students may meet and surpass the standards: 1) structures; 2) basic principles; 3) teambuilding and classbuilding; 4) teams; 5) man-

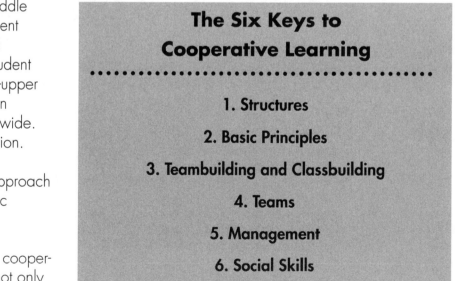

The Six Keys to Cooperative Learning

1. Structures

2. Basic Principles

3. Teambuilding and Classbuilding

4. Teams

5. Management

6. Social Skills

agement; and (6) social skills. In Chapter 8, we will revisit structures and provide more concrete examples of how structures may be used to deliver science curriculum to reach the science standards.

The Six Keys to Successful Cooperative Learning
Key 1: Structures
The basic premise of Kagan Cooperative Learning is that there is a strong relation between what students do and what students learn. That is, interactions in the classroom have a profound effect on the social, cognitive, and academic development of students. The construction and acquisition of knowledge, the development of language and cognition, and the development of social skills are largely a function of the situations in which students interact.

For this reason, a major direction of the structural approach has been to quantify classroom interactions and to analyze them in terms of their effects on the students. This analysis has led to the development of step-by-step structures, ways to structure the interaction among students and how they interact with the curriculum. The Kagan structures are the essential tools for teachers to direct the interaction of students in ways which will result in a range of learning outcomes. It is relatively easy for teachers and students to learn these social interaction sequences,

No single instructional strategy can successfully reach all the standards. Cooperative learning opens a world of possibilities.

called "structures." Put simply, a structure describes exactly how the students (and sometimes the teacher) are to interact with each other and process the curriculum. There are many different structures. Just as the standards range from the mastery of very discrete skills to higher-level understanding of processes, so too do the structures range from those designed to master discrete skills to those designed to foster higher-level thinking. No single instructional strategy can successfully accomplish the range of learning objectives established by the standards, so there are a range of structures.

Recent work in applying brain research and research on multiple intelligences to the classroom provides support for using a range of structures. The cooperative structures provide a safe context for learning — a context in which downshifting is less likely. The multimodal structures make learning more engaging, meaningful, and provide more windows onto the curriculum. We think of the structures as tools in a teacher's toolbox. When it is time to build learning experiences for our students, we pull from our toolbox the appropriate structures to create the desired learning outcomes.

Key 2: Basic Principles
There are four basic principles central to the Kagan Structural Approach of cooperative learning, summarized by the acronym PIES: Positive Interdependence, Individual Accountability, Equal Participation, and Simul-

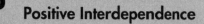

PIES: The Basic Principles of Cooperative Learning

P   Positive Interdependence

I   Individual Accountability

E   Equal Participation

S   Simultaneous Interaction

taneous Interaction. These principles are discussed in detail (Kagan, 1994; Kagan and Kagan, 1993). The inclusion of these basic principles in the structuring of learning tasks facilitates reaching high academic standards. For that reason, all of the structures advocated in the Kagan approach to cooperative learning incorporate these principles. That is, structures have the basic principles "built in."

1. Positive Interdependence

Positive Interdependence is the most basic principle in cooperative learning. Positive Interdependence is created whenever a gain for one means a gain for another or when help is necessary. Two individuals are mutually positively interdependent if the gains of each helps the other. Two powerful forces are released when we make students positively interdependent academically: If any student needs help, he or she finds among his teammates or classmates willing tutors (a gain for one is a gain for the other); and students are encouraged by their teammates and classmates to do their very best, raising motivation.

Positive Interdependence is created within structures in various ways — usually not by the inclusion of one element, but rather by a sequence of elements. For example, let's look at a Three-Step Interview. In the first two steps, teammates are in pairs interviewing each other both ways. In the third step, students tell their teammates what they learned from their partner in the interview. The teammates have no other way of obtaining the information, so they are dependent on the interviewing, listening, and speaking skills of their teammate. Thus, this third step creates positive interdependence; help is necessary and the better each student is at interviewing, listening, and sharing, the more each will learn — a gain for one is a gain for the others.

Let's take another example. In Numbered Heads Together, after the teacher asks a question, the students are given time to put their heads together to make sure their teammates all know the answer. At that stage, if any student knows, it increases the probability that the teammates will learn — a gain for one is a gain for the others. Further, students know that following the team discussion, only one number is chosen. If that teammate does well, his/her gain is a gain for the others. Thus each team member wants all of their teammates to do well.

2. Individual Accountability

Individual accountability is making each member accountable for his or her own learning or contribution. For example, in Numbered Heads Together, over time each student is held accountable to the teacher and classmates for sharing an answer or idea. The element that holds students accountable is the last step of Numbered Heads Together: students share with the class. When it is made clear to the students that they are being held accountable, it increases the likelihood that they will listen and participate. If, for instance, Numbered Heads Together was modified to exclude the last step, students would know that they are not accountable for sharing an answer, and some might not pay attention at all.

Similarly, in Three-Step Interview, students are held accountable to the team for the information they receive from a teammate during an interview. Because students know they will be held accountable, they listen intently. Individual accountability is also "built-in" to Kagan structures so there is not a diffusion of responsibility. Students are each individually accountable for their own learning.

3. Equal Participation

Simultaneous Interaction does quite well to get students actively involved. When we do Teams Discuss rather than Class Discusses, one in four students is speaking rather than one in about 30. But if we look closely at what is happening in our team discussion, we may find that one outspoken student is doing all the talking while the teammates are doing all the listening. This is not Equal Participation. To make sure everyone has an equal chance to speak, we might have each teammate in turn share with the team (a RoundRobin) rather than use Teams Discuss. Now every student has an equal role in sharing information.

What would we do if we wanted to have our class answer a series of questions about the basic features of the Earth? We know there would be more involvement if students answered the questions in their teams than if the teacher called to the board one student at a time to answer a question. But if we just tell the team to solve the problems, we would find once again one or two students doing most or all of the problems. If we make it clear, however, that the students are to use a structure like RoundTable or RallyTable (each in turn solves one problem), then each student will participate nearly equally.

Similarly, during a pair discussion focused on recalling the steps of an experiment, one student may do all the talking. To equalize participation, we may have students take turns sharing with a partner (a RallyRobin), alternating turns describing one step.

Cooperative learning structures are powerful tools to reach high academic standards. An understanding of the basic principles enhances teacher effectiveness.

As a general rule, we want to make sure that our students participate roughly equally. The Kagan structures have "built-in" equal participation that ensure all of our students are active participants in the learning process.

4. Simultaneous Interaction

Interaction may occur simultaneously or sequentially. Sequential interaction occurs when students participate one at a time, in a sequence, taking turns. If one person at a time is called upon to share an idea, the interaction is sequential. Sequential interaction is limiting and inefficient. To give each student in a class of 30 one minute to share ideas using a one-at-a-time structure takes about thirty minutes.

Simultaneous Interaction occurs in a classroom when there is more than one active participant at a time. Simultaneous interaction is usually preferable to sequential interaction because it increases the number of students actively involved at any one moment, increasing the amount of active participation time per student. To give each student one minute to share if students are taking turns talking in pairs, takes only two minutes. Pair work is a simultaneous structure because the action is taking place simultaneously in many places all at the same time.

Let's look at a discussion. When we have some issue to discuss in the classroom, we have alternatives as to how it may be discussed. We can use Class Discusses, Teams Discuss, or Pairs Discuss. If active participation is our primary objective, applying the Simultaneity Prin-

ciple, we would choose a Teams Discuss over a Class Discusses, and a Pairs Discuss over a Teams Discuss. In Class Discusses, there is one person speaking at a time; in Teams Discuss, on the average one person in each team is talking at any one moment, so one quarter of the class is talking at a time; and in Pairs Discuss, half the class is actively expressing ideas at any one moment.

What about presentations? If teams have prepared presentations and it is time for them to share with the class, what element would we use? We could use Team Presents to the Class. If the presentation was five minutes and it took about a minute for transitions, it would take 48 minutes for eight teams to present to the class. Applying the Simultaneity Principle, we instead choose Teams Present to Teams. If every team made their five-minute presentation to another team, took a minute for transition, and then the presenting team became the receiving team, in 11 minutes every team will have given and received a presentation. This leaves us with plenty of time for teams to reflect, discuss their presentations, and fine tune them. Then they can try them again with another team as a new audience. Notice that by applying the Simultaneity Principle we can accomplish more than twice as much in less than half the time!

Key 3: Teambuilding & Classbuilding

What appears like time-off task can be viewed as a very important investment in creating the social context necessary for teams to maximize their potential. Again and again, we have observed greater long-run learning as well as liking of class, school, and subject matter when teachers take time for teambuilding and classbuilding. When there is a positive team identity, liking, respect, and trust among team members and classmates, there is a context within which maximum learning can occur. Teambuilding and classbuilding are brain compatible; they create the safe classroom in which higher-order cognitive functioning may occur. By investing in creating a positive classroom environment, we provide a classroom in which the standards are more likely to be achieved by all students.

When teambuilding and classbuilding are neglected, especially in classrooms in which there are preexisting tensions, teams experience serious difficulties. Kagan (1994) distinguishes five aims of teambuilding and classbuilding and provides structures appropriate for each. The five aims of teambuilding are: (1) Getting Acquainted, (2) Team Identity, (3) Mutual Support, (4) Valuing Differences, and (5) Developing Synergy. In the books *Teambuilding* (Kagan et al., 1997) and *Classbuilding* (Kagan et al., 1995), a range of structures are used to create a caring, cooperative classroom environment as well as to build effective learning teams. Lessons are provided in the book *Communitybuilding* for creating an inclusive classroom environment using cooperative learning structures (Shaw, 1992).

Teambuilding can be fun, success-for-all, activities such as creating a team handshake or banner. Not all team-

Teambuilding and classbuilding establish a positive team and class environment. Academic learning flourishes in the caring, cooperative classroom.

building, however, is time off from academic work. There are many content-related teambuilding activities which serve the dual purposes of uniting the team as well as providing an anticipatory set and/or distributed practice in a lesson. In the structural approach we encourage the use of content-related teambuilding. For example, students might play with the content by using RoundTable to list as many things as they can that are made from metal. Alternatively, they might use 4S Brainstorming to generate as many explanations as possible for why water takes up more volume when frozen than when in a liquid form.

If the cooperative learning lesson is simple and fun, as with the Flashcard Game or Numbered Heads Together, usually little or no teambuilding is necessary. If, on the other hand, the lesson involves activities in which conflicts might arise (choosing a topic or format for a project), it is important that a strong, and positive team identity is developed prior to the lesson.

Classbuilding provides networking among all of the students in a class and creates a positive context within which teams can learn. Although students spend most of their time in teams in the cooperative classroom, it is important that students see themselves as part of a larger supportive group — the class — not just as members of one small team.

Key 4: Teams
What Is a Team?

A cooperative learning team has a strong, positive team identity, ideally consists of four members, and endures over time. Teammates know and accept each other and provide mutual support. Ability to establish a variety of types of cooperative learning teams is a key competency of a cooperative learning teacher. "Teams" may be contrasted with "groups," which do not necessarily endure over time or have an identity. Kagan (1994) distinguishes four major types of cooperative learning teams and assorted methods to produce them. The four most common cooperative arrangements are: (1) Heterogeneous Teams, (2) Random Groups, (3) Interest Teams, and (4) Homogeneous Language Teams. Each of these types of teams is useful for different purposes.

The most common cooperative learning teamformation methods group students to maximize heterogeneity. The heterogeneous team is a mirror of the classroom, including, to the extent possible, high, middle, and low achievers, boys and girls, and an ethnic and linguistic diversity. Heterogeneity of achievement levels maximizes positive peer tutoring and serves as an aid to classroom management. With a high achiever on each team, introduction and acquisition of new material becomes easier. Mixed ethnicity dramatically improves ethnic relations among students. The heterogeneous team also makes classroom management easier

Working in teams improves academic achievement, ethnic relations, self-esteem, and liking for class and school.

— having a high achiever on each team can be like having one teacher aide for every three students.

If we always use heterogeneous teams, however, the high achievers would never interact (missing important academic stimulation) and the low achievers would never be on the same team (missing leadership opportunities). Thus, there is a need for additional team formation methods. Nonheterogeneous teams can be formed in a variety of ways, including self-selection (allowing students to group themselves by friendships or interests) or random selection (students draw a number from 1 to 8 for team assignments). Self-selection runs a strong risk of promoting or reinforcing status hierarchies in the classroom ("in" and "out"groups); random selection runs the risk of the creation of "loser" teams (the four lowest achievers in the classroom may end up on the same team if it is left to the luck of the draw). There are important benefits, however, derived from the occasional use of random, interest, or homogeneous language teams. In the structural approach, teachers are encouraged to learn the domain of usefulness of a range of team formation methods and to choose the method most appropriate for the objectives at hand.

How Are Teams Formed?

There are a variety of methods of team formation. Students can group themselves by friendships or interests, random teams may be formed by the luck of the draw, or teachers can assign students to teams. Kagan and

Robertson (1992) provide a Teamformation Kit based on "T-cards" and a "T-card Holder," which allow easy assignment and reassignment of heterogeneous teams as well as record keeping of prior assignments.

How Long Should Teams Stay Together?
If random team formation methods are used, in most classrooms teams must be changed frequently — every day or so because of the possibility of the four lowest achievers in the class ending up on the same team. If teams are carefully designed by the teacher, they can stay together for a long time and students can learn how to learn together. We suggest changing heterogeneous teams after five or six weeks, even if they are functioning well. This enables students to transfer their new social and academic skills to new situations.

How Big Should Teams Be?
Teams of four are ideal. They allow pair work which doubles participation and opens twice as many lines of communication compared with teams of three. Teams larger than four often do not lead to enough participation and they are harder to manage. Much of the rationale for cooperative learning is based on the benefits of active participation. As the group size is made smaller, active participation increases. As students share in a group of eight, 1/8 of the class is an active participant at any one time. Groups of four allow 1/4 of the class to produce language at any one time — from the

perspective of active participation, they are twice as good as groups of eight.

Given this rationale, why not move to groups of three or even pairs? There are three reasons why teams of four are most effective. (1) Pair work doubles the amount of participation. With groups of three there is an odd-student-out while doing pair work. Pairs Check, Paired Reading, and the Flashcard Game are among the structures which maximize simultaneous interaction through pair work. (2) The social psychology of a group of three is often a pair and an outsider. Two people hit it off well and talk to each other often, leaving one left out. (3) Compared with a group of three, a group of four doubles the probability of an optimum cognitive and linguistic mismatch. Both the Piagetian moral development work and linguistic development work indicates that we learn well from someone only somewhat different from our own level of development — someone who will provide stimulation in our zone of proximal development. In a group of three there are three possible pairs; in a group of four, there are six.

Key 5: Management
Many teachers report that their management problems decrease dramatically once they switch to cooperative learning. The reason is that in the traditional classroom

> *Cooperative learning meets some of students' most basic needs: The need to belong and the need to interact. Effective classroom management is essential to channel the released energy.*

there is a mismatch between the needs of the students and the structure of the classroom. The nature of a student is active and interactive: Students want to "do" and to talk. And the traditional classroom demands that students be passive and isolated. Naturally, the students do not give up their basic needs without a struggle. And so a great deal of energy is spent keeping the students in their seats, "not bothering their neighbors," and quiet. The cooperative classroom, in contrast, is better aligned with the needs of students. It is based on the assumption that learning occurs through doing and interacting. Students are encouraged to interact, move, create, and do. Feeling their basic needs met, students are no longer "management problems."

Nevertheless, there are a number of management skills necessary in the cooperative classroom which are not involved in managing a traditional classroom. Cooperative classroom management differs radically from classroom management in the traditional classroom. In the traditional classroom, managing student behavior means instituting a system to keep students from talking or interacting. In contrast, in the cooperative classroom student-student interaction is encouraged and so management involves different skills. Some of the management concerns introduced along with the introduction of teams include seating arrangement, noise level, giving directions, distribution and storage of team materials, and methods of shaping the behavior of groups.

The teacher establishes a quiet signal which at any time quickly focuses all attention away from peer interaction and toward the teacher. Extensive use of teacher and student modeling is an efficient cooperative management technique, as is extensive use of structuring. Efficient methods of distributing materials are established; for example, selecting a Materials Monitor for each team. The room is arranged so that each student has equal and easy access to each teammate (ideally, each student on a team can easily put both hands on a common piece of paper) and all students are able to easily and comfortably orient themselves toward the teacher and blackboard. Cooperative classroom management is explored in depth in *Cooperative Learning* (Kagan, 1994).

Increasing emphasis is being placed on life skills, character development, and emotional intelligence. The push to meet academic standards must be balanced with other essential skills. Cooperative learning empowers teachers to develop academic and social skills in tandem.

Key 6: Social Skills

Research reveals that with no social skills instruction at all, students in cooperative teams become more caring, helpful, and understanding of each other. This can be seen as a positive by-product of students working together successfully. Although social skills are not emphasized in specific curriculum standards, they are of primary importance in a range of standards publications dealing with life skills (for example, What Work Requires of Schools: A SCANS Report for America 2000 and Workplace Basics: The Essential Skills Employers Want). Separate life skills classes and add-on social skill units are not a reality for most schools and classrooms struggling to achieve the other curriculum standards. It is overwhelming. If we do value these skills, wish to deliver a differentiated social skills curriculum, and strive to have our teams and classrooms run as efficiently as possible, we cannot depend entirely on the natural acquisition of social skills.

One alternative is the Structured Natural Approach (Kagan, 1994) in which teachers structure so students acquire social skills while they are doing their math, or science, or social studies with little time off the regular curriculum. Teachers using the approach actually cover more of the academic curriculum than those who do not, because their classes function smoothly: There is little time lost as students keep themselves on task, give efficient help to each other, and monitor and adjust their own noise levels.

The Structured Natural Approach for social skills acquisition uses four tools: (1) Roles & Gambits, (2) Modeling & Reinforcement, (3) Structures & Structuring, and (4) Reflection & Planning Time. As the students interact in their cooperative groups, they become skillful in listening, paraphrasing, taking the role of the other, managing group processes, and dealing with the dominant, shy, hostile, and withdrawn group members. They acquire skills, not just learn about skills.

Resources

Johnson, D. W., G. Maruyama, R. Johnson, D. Nelson, L. & Skon. *Effects of cooperative, competitive and individualistic goal structures on achievement: a meta-analysis.* Psychological Bulletin, 1981, 89, 47–62.

Kagan, L., M. Kagan, & S. Kagan. *Teambuilding.* San Clemente, CA: Kagan Publishing, 1995.

Kagan, M. & S. Kagan. *Advanced Cooperative Learning: Playing with Elements.* San Clemente, CA: Kagan Publishing, 1993.

Kagan, M., L. Kagan, & S. Kagan. *Classbuilding.* San Clemente, CA: Kagan Publishing, 1995.

Kagan, Spencer. *Cooperative Learning.* San Clemente, CA: Kagan Publishing, 1994.

Kagan, Spencer. *Dimensions of Cooperative Classroom Structures* in *Learning to Cooperate, Cooperating to Learn.* New York, NY: Plenum Press, 1985.

Kagan, S., & L. Kagan. *Teamformation Pocket Chart.* San Clemente, CA: Kagan Publishing, 1992.

Shaw, Vanston. *Communitybuilding.* San Clemente, CA: Kagan Publishing, 1992.

Reaching the Standards:
Students with Disabilities

Reaching

the standards with a class full of differently abled students is a challenging task for general education teachers. Classrooms almost always include a diverse group of students. Students vary widely on how they learn, the rate at which they learn, and how they display their learning. The challenge of reaching the standards is compounded by the inclusion of students with disabilities in general education classrooms. Let's face it: Reaching the standards for all is not an easy task. However, the alternative to inclusion — the segregation of students by personal characteristics — is far less attractive. Sorting, labeling, segregating, and tracking students, performed under the false pretenses of effectiveness and expediency, are perhaps the most insidious practices of modern American education. There is an alternative. An alternative that works!

In this chapter, we illustrate the increasing pressure for inclusion and the necessity for effective classroom practices. We discuss the philosophical basis for inclusion: the basic unfairness of separate, not equal programs. We then argue, with substantial supporting research, that inclusion is good not only for students with disabilities, but also for their classmates without disabilities. Then we focus on some of the practical issues of inclusion: The special adaptations and modifications necessary to achieve the standards. And most importantly, on how cooperative learning and the creation of an inclusive classroom environment is effective for all students.

Increasing Pressure for Inclusion

Effective practices for inclusion are becoming increasingly important due to the increase in numbers of special needs students placed in general education classrooms. Increased school enrollments, an increase in the identification of students with disabilities, and the inclusion legislation has general education teachers teaching more students with special needs each year.

Inclusion Law

Letter of Inclusion Law

"...to the maximum extent appropriate, handicapped children, including those children in public and private institutions or other care facilities, are educated with children who are not handicapped, and that special classes, separate schooling, or other removal of handicapped children from the regular educational environment occurs only when the nature or severity of the handicap is such that education in regular classes with the use of supplementary aids and services cannot be achieved satisfactorily."
— *Public Law 101-476; Section 1412 [5][B]*

Spirit of Inclusion Law

All children should learn together.

Necessary supports and services should be provided to help children with disabilities be successful in regular classes.

According to the U.S. Department of Education, the number of special needs children ages 6 to 12 has increased 25.3 percent in 10 years. Children ages 12 to 17 with special needs have increased 30.7 percent in the same period. In the 1996–1997 school year there were 5.8 million 3- to 21-year-olds with disabilities — accounting for 10.8 percent of the nation's total enrollment. The Individuals with Disabilities Education Act (IDEA) or Public Law 105-17 as reauthorized in 1997 provided a definite emphasis on inclusion of these special needs students in regular classrooms. It was a clear directive that all students, no matter what their category of disability, should have access to the regular curriculum.

The Philosophy of Inclusion

The most compelling argument for inclusion is that differential treatment of students is simply unfair! The landmark court case Brown v. Board of Education in 1954 made a resounding resolution: Separate is not equal! Students of all races, sexes, colors, creeds, and levels of ability should have the same opportunity and the same access to the core curriculum. A separate education potentially provides students with differential curricula, instruction, and lowered expectations. The prevailing achievement ideology in our nation, and a defining characteristic of greatness, is that regardless of background or socioeconomic status, it is the right of every citizen in our democracy to have equal access to a quality education. Education is seen as the great equalizer. We cannot therefore preferentially deny students access to the highest standards of public education. The standards and curriculum set forth by our nation, state, district, and

schools are for all. The ethical solution is to provide all students equal access to the curriculum. This means students with disabilities should not be denied access to the same high standards as students without disabilities. Differential treatment of students is unfair and violates the most basic tenet of education in our democracy: equal access to a quality education.

Research on Inclusion

Does the principle of equal access apply to students with disabilities? If differentiated curricula and instruction were found to be more effective than equal access, then perhaps we could argue that this form of segregation was warranted. However, this is not the case. In fact, just the opposite may be true.

Special Programs Are Less Effective than Inclusion

Researchers have compared the effectiveness of special pull-out programs to the placement of students with disabilities in regular classrooms. Findings indicate that students with disabilities are better off being placed in regular classrooms than in special pull-out programs. Very few studies indicate any positive effects for segregating students over inclusion in regular classrooms and many indicate inclusion is more effective (Lipsky & Gartner, 1989; Meyer & Putnam, 1988). In a review of 50 studies comparing the academic achievement of students with disabilities in regular versus special programs, there was a 30 percentile difference, favoring inclusion in regular classroom over segregation (Weiner, 1985). More recent meta-analyses report students perform better academically and socially in inclu-

The Rationale for Inclusion

• Help all students reach the standards
• Improve academic achievement for all
• Nurture the development of social skills
• Increase student expectations
• Eliminate discrimination
• Develop social skills of students without disabilities
• Provide equal opportunity for all students
• Equalize access to core curriculum
• Provide age-appropriate classroom settings
• Foster self-esteem through individual learning success
• Encourage cooperation among teachers
• Enhance diversity skills
• Provide opportunity for family participation in local schools

sive general education classroom settings than in pull-out programs (Baker, Wang, & Walberg, 1994, 1995). If our goal is to help all students achieve success both academically and socially, then the value of inclusion cannot be overstated. Inclusion is essential for providing equal educational opportunity for all students and for helping all students reach high standards.

Inclusion Holds Benefits for Students Without Disabilities

Studies, although limited, suggest nondisabled students also benefit from inclusion. In our increasingly pluralistic society, the ability to get along with and work with others who look and act differently is an essential life skill. Through classroom interactions with differently abled students, especially positively interdependent cooperative interactions, regular students develop social and emotional skills. The benefits for students without disabilities include:

• Improved academic performance through tutoring
• Improved attitude toward students with disabilities
• Reduced fear of differences
• Increased ability to perform in heterogeneous situations
• Development of respect, tolerance, patience, caring, and cooperation virtues
• Increased self-esteem
• Improved leadership skills
• Development of social skills

Cooperative Learning and Inclusion

A positive implication of using cooperative learning strategies in the classroom is that cooperative learning can be both a modification and an adaptation. The use of specific structures allows students to provide answers in formats other than the traditional paper and pencil method. It also allows the instructor to check for understanding in ways that do not isolate a special needs student as the only student participating in a nontraditional style.

Research on Cooperative Learning and Inclusion

The effects of the use of cooperative learning have been extensively studied with disabled students. Reviews by Slavin (1990, 1995), Johnson et al. (1981), and Johnson and Johnson (1989) find cooperative learning more effective than individualistic and competitive learning for increasing academic performance and social acceptance of students with disabilities. Students who worked cooperatively were also found to have a greater liking for students with and without disabilities than students who worked in other learning situations. The strongest and most consistent effects occur with the basic principles of individual accountability and positive interdependence in place.

The National Center on Educational Restructuring and Inclusion (NCERI), an organization established to promote and support educational programs where all students are served effectively in inclusive settings, conducts national studies to identify the key factors in successful inclusion programs by practicing school districts. NCERI reports cooperative learning is identified as the most important instructional strategy for including students in the regular classroom:

> The data indicate that instructional strategies and classroom practices that support inclusive education for the most part are the same ones that teachers believe are effective

for students in general. They report that a precursor to inclusive programs is a belief in the benefits of heterogeneous classrooms. Of the districts reporting, cooperative learning is identified as the most important instructional strategy supporting inclusive education. (NCERI, 1995)

Adaptations and Modifications for Inclusion

In the past, students with disabilities have been removed from classrooms in favor of separate educational programs. This practice may cause more harm than good. The alternative is to provide adaptations and modification to the instruction and curriculum to accommodate special needs students. The law included wording to state that "appropriate adaptations and modifications" should be made for the student.

Of the districts reporting, cooperative learning is identified as the most important instructional strategy supporting inclusive education.

- **Adaptations** can be thought of as changes to the environment, access changes, or a differentiated manner in which a student can demonstrate knowledge of a subject with adapted expectations or materials (e.g., while the team is calculating how long it would take to travel from planet to planet at given speeds, a student on an adapted curriculum may be figuring the distances between planets).

- **Modifications** usually mean that the method of instruction, outcome, expectations, and/or materials differ significantly from the other students' in the classroom. In this case the student may be working on a parallel activity (e.g., while the class is working on difficult vocabulary words, student is working on words at the appropriate level of difficulty).

When any child with a disability is being included in a regular classroom it is important to complete a learning and environmental assessment. A physically disabled child should be observed and assessed by an occupational and physical therapist. It is amazing what minor adaptations to the physical setting can do to assist the success of a disabled student. If your district has assistive and adaptive technology personnel, they can provide ideas for adapting the environment and providing curriculum access. The visually and hearing impaired students can also be made more successful if the regular education teacher understands proximity, use of specialized equipment, and some ideas on general cues in the classroom during instruction.

Cooperative learning and flexible activities, that are integral aspects of instruction in our inclusive primary classroom, make inclusion easier. Our students are able to participate easily in small group activities and participate in individualized outcomes.
— *Pulaki County Schools, KY (NCERI, 1995)*

General Adaptations and Modifications

Adaptations and modifications may be essential components to successful inclusion. Some general alterations to consider when including a student with disabilities in the regular classroom include:

1. Workload
2. Difficulty
3. Time
4. Support
5. Teaching Strategies
6. Student Responses
7. Participation

Other instructional strategies cited by a quarter or more of the districts in the NCERI report (1995) include:

- curricular modifications
- "hands-on" teaching (especially in science and mathematics)
- whole language instruction
- use of peers as tutors and "buddies"
- thematic and multidisciplinary curriculum
- the use of paraprofessional/classroom aides
- the use of instructional technology

Cooperative Learning Adaptations

In the cooperative learning classroom, special adaptations are helpful in assisting students with disabilities to maximize academic performance. Teachers who instruct special needs students should be part of the creation of the individualized education plan (IEP). This document

Adaptations & Modifications for Inclusion

1. Workload

Adapt the amount of work required. Individualize the task for students with disabilities.

• *Example: Special needs student is required to look up the definition of four vocabulary words; other students are required to look up more.*

2. Difficulty

Adapt the skill level required. The difficulty of the task should be adjusted to the student's personal objective.

• *Example: Special needs student may be conducting a simpler experiment than other students. Special needs student may list outcomes in order of size; other students may be required to show results using a pie or line graph.*

3. Time

Adapt the time allotted for completing a task or for learning materials. Students with disabilities may require different completion rates.

• *Example: Special needs student is given more time to complete assignment.*

4. Support

Provide increased personal support and materials. Personal support may include: instructional aides, specialists, or parents. Support materials may include: books on tape, visuals, manipulatives, braille material.

• *Example: An aide signs the teacher's speech for hearing disabled student.*

5. Teaching Strategies

Adapt the teaching strategy. Use multimodal strategies to provide multiple modes of accessing the curriculum. Actively involve students with peers.

• *Example: Use cooperative learning so special needs student interacts with classmates over content in a positive way.*

6. Student Responses

Adapt the type of responses required from students. Students with certain disabilities will not be able to respond in the same way as other students. Some types of responses include: writing, speaking, reading, looking, pointing, moving manipulatives, drawing, painting, singing, dancing, or demonstrating. Select appropriate response modes for students with disabilities.

• *Example: Allow special needs student to answer questions verbally rather than in writing, or to select from pre-made response cards rather than writing answers.*

7. Participation

Adapt the type of participation required.

• *Example: Allow special needs student to fill a realistic role for the team project.*

identifies the type of modifications that are needed across settings. When using cooperative learning, teachers are advised to make the IEP team aware that cooperative learning is an integral part of the classroom environment. This will focus discussion on what accommodations may be needed. This includes the student with significant behavior needs. A student who needs instruction in behavior should have a plan as part of the IEP. If cooperative learning is being used as an instructional tool then the goals should focus on the types of behaviors that would allow the student to be successful in the group interactions.

Preparing Students for Inclusion

One of the most powerful ways in which cooperative learning can be successful with students with special needs is gambit development among teammates and classmates. Gambits are the functional phrases and actions which allow us to accomplish goals in social interaction situations. For example, some interruption gambits are "Can you pardon me

Cooperative learning and active learning techniques are prominent instructional practices that support inclusion.
— *Baltimore City Schools (NCERI, 1995)*

for a moment, please?" and "If you will excuse me, what I need to know is…" Some praising gambits are "What I really liked about what you just did is…" and "Great job!" Regular education students are often unprepared with what to do or say with a teammate who cannot write, who has emotional outbursts, whose attention is wandering, or who often does not understand instructions. Teachers who take the time to teach gambits for dealing successfully with others who have special needs reap two kinds of benefits: The student with special needs is surrounded by others who are willing to offer help and support, and the other students learn a caring, helping, and supportive orientation. The will to help is released through gambit development. In the absence of gambit development, the student with special needs is often ignored or even shunned. Putting down the student with special needs is a way of masking one's own inadequacy. Empowered with the appropriate gambits, students will approach and deal successfully with others, a two-way win. There are a number of approaches to gambit development. See box: Gambits to Meet Special Needs.

Adaptations of Cooperative Learning Structures

Special adaptations and accommodations for the cooperative learning structures described in this Teacher's Guide and video series are provided in Chapter 8. These adaptations increase the likelihood of successful inclusion of students with disabilities when implementing the cooperative learning structures.

Gambits to Meet Special Needs

Recognizing that students do not know what to do or say when a teammate is not paying attention, the teacher may address the whole class and say something like this: "Class, all of us have our attention wander sometimes. When that happens, we appreciate it if those around us can help us refocus on the task at hand. What are some of the things others can say or do, if our attention wanders?"

The class then generates a list of gambits to deal with attention deficit, such as:
- "Susie, we are trying to build X. Do you think we should put this piece here or over here?"
- "Johnnie, we are deciding how to do our team presentation. I would like to know your idea. Do you like the idea of a skit or a TV quiz show better?"
- "Frank, I would really like to hear your idea on that. Do you agree with X or with Y?"

Physical Needs
"May I move the piece for you?"
"Would you like me to write down your idea on that?"
"Let me get that for you."

Cognitive Needs
"May I read it to you?"
"Let me see if I can build that with manipulatives for you."
"How about if I draw it."

Behavioral or Emotional Needs
Support:
"Don't worry about making a mistake, we all make mistakes. That is how we learn."
"I'm glad to have you as a teammate."

Encouragement:
"Take your time, we are in no rush."
"Your answer will be just fine."

Praise:
"Great job!"
"I liked it when you…"

Attention:
"Let's all focus on…"
"Pete, what do you think of…"

Anger:
"We all get angry sometimes. Let's take some time to cool down."
"It is frustrating to keep working on a difficult problem. Let's do some easier problems and come back to these later."

Hyperactivity:
"Let's keep discussing it, but let's walk as we do."
"How about doing a few rounds of Turn Toss as we give answers."

Tension:
"Let's practice taking some deep breaths and letting them out slowly."
"How about our practicing some muscle relaxation?"

Due to the spectrum of potential disabilities, it would be impossible to list a specific accommodation for each disability category for each structure. Therefore, we have grouped student disabilities into three broad categories: A) Physical Disabilities, B) Cognitive Disabilities, and C) Behavioral or Emotional Disabilities. In Chapter 8, where appropriate, specific adaptations are provided for each structure for each category of disability. We provide some general guidelines for allowing all students to participate to the fullest extent of their ability. The very nature of cooperative learning allows a higher level of participation for all students and with some basic changes the structures are even more beneficial to provide enhanced learning experiences.

The Power of PIES

The four basic principles to Kagan cooperative learning (PIES) were described in detail in Chapter 4. Kagan structures have these principles built in. The use of cooperative learning structures integrates these basic principles and enhances inclusion:

• Positive Interdependence
There is increased helping, tutoring, caring, and cooperation because students are positively interdependent. Students feel they are on the same team because a gain for a teammate is a gain for their team. In many structures, help is required by all for successful task completion.

Three Categories of Disabilities
• •

Category A:
Physical Disabilities
This category includes students that have access issues, such as:
- Significant communication/speech, vision, or hearing disorders.
- Wheelchair-bound, spasticity of muscles, paralysis.
- Seizure disorders; balance or gait disorders.

Category B:
Cognitive Disabilities
This includes a broad range of students, from students with learning disabilities through those with mental retardation, such as:
- Short- or long-term memory deficit, traumatic brain injury, limited attention span, impaired concentration.
- Impairments of communication, perception, planning, sequencing, reading, and writing skills.

Category C:
Behavioral or Emotional Disabilities
This includes a broad range of students ranging from those with attention deficit disorders to severe emotional disability, such as:
- Lowered self-esteem, lack of motivation, inability to cope, anxiety.
- Inability to self-monitor behavior; difficulty in relating and socializing with others.
- Self-centeredness, depression, sexual dysfunctions.

• Individual Accountability

Although students work together in teams, each individual is held accountable for their own learning. Individual accountability is crucial for inclusion for two reasons. First, individual accountability counters the trend toward a diffusion of responsibility. Through various structures, students are held accountable for listening, sharing, writing, and coaching. Active participation increases learning. Second, individual accountability reduces tension when working with students with disabilities. Since students are held individually accountable for their own learning, students are not evaluated based on the performance of a student with a disability.

• Equal Participation

Everyone must participate about equally. Through cooperative structures with built-in equal participation, students with disabilities are truly included in the team and are given the opportunity to participate.

• Simultaneous Interaction

All students are actively involved. Active involvement boosts motivation and learning.

Cooperative learning is one strategy that supports inclusion. Another is peer tutoring. Where they are being used, inclusion is successful.
— Franklin Northeast Supervisory Union, VT (NCERI, 1995)

Creating the Inclusive Classroom

Cooperative learning is the embodiment of the inclusive philosophy. Mainstreaming without cooperative learning is not inclusion. There is a dramatic difference between just being placed in a classroom and being a member of a team. Through cooperative learning students are truly included in the learning process.

Further, cooperative learning transforms the classroom orientation. The classroom becomes more caring, cooperative, and amenable to inclusion. Students in the cooperative learning classroom develop a more prosocial, inclusive orientation towards students with or without disabilities. It is within this classroom context that inclusion becomes a reality. Students are accepted for their disabilities. Students come to focus not on the disability, but rather on students' strengths, how a student can use his or her abilities, and how classmates and teammates can help them play an important part on the team.

In the process of working together in teams, students with disabilities are not nominally included in regular classrooms. They become true members of a team and of the class. The effectiveness of team functioning and classroom climate is largely enhanced by teambuilding, classbuilding, and communitybuilding. Through inclusive activities, students feel a sense of belonging on their teams and in their classroom. They create mutual support. And in this nonthreatening inclusive environment, all students are more free to reach their academic potential.

Placing a student with disabilities in a regular classroom is not inclusion. With no special preparation, the other students are likely to ignore or even make fun of the newcomer. It is instinctual for students to group with and become friends with those who are like them, those with whom they feel a connection. It is only the very exceptional student who will reach out to someone who on the surface appears different. Thus, with few exceptions, mainstreaming a student with special needs without special preparations fails to create inclusion — and often creates the opposite of an inclusive experience.

Cooperative learning is the special preparation needed to create meaningful inclusion. Through cooperative learning students come to value and need a contribution from each teammate. They learn what to do or say if a teammate is having difficulties. They learn how to see and work beyond a disability so a student with a disability can express him/herself and live up to his/her potential. With cooperative learning in place, students make connections with each other. Students see beyond disabilities and come to see each other for who they are.

Concluding Remarks

Inclusion presents educators with a great challenge. We know from the research that pull-out and self-contained placements are not as effective as regular classrooms for students with special needs. For these students, inclusion supports academic achievement, peer acceptance, and self-esteem. We know also that regular students benefit from their interactions with students of special needs, gaining diversity skills as well as positive character virtues and facets of emotional intelligence such as empathy, caring, responsibility, and citizenship skills. The question, then, is not whether we should have inclusion. The question is how best to structure inclusion.

Positive inclusion experiences do not result from placing students with special needs into regular classrooms and hoping for the best. Only by carefully structuring the inclusion experience can we maximize the positive impact. That is where cooperative learning comes in. Cooperative learning, when carefully structured, is the very embodiment of the inclusive educational philosophy. Research on cooperative learning has shown that for disabled students there are positive outcomes in both academic achievement and social acceptance. On the other side, regular students show increases in social acceptance and caring.

There are many forms of cooperative learning and many adaptations which can be made to better meet the needs of all students. Among the most effective adaptations for students with special needs are modifications which adjust workload, task difficulty, time, teaching strategies, response modes, and roles in groups. One of the most powerful of all methods is to empower all students with gambits (what to say or do) to meet the special needs of their teammates.

Research supports the most fundamental principle of democratic educational philosophy: Equal opportunity for all students. Research reveals that separate programs do not provide equal opportunity. But inclusion without cooperative learning is not really inclusion either. Only when inclusion classrooms have carefully structured cooperative learning teams, with teammates well-prepared to deal with the special needs of their fellow students, can we then realize the dream of each student maximizing his/her potential.

Resources

Baker, E. T., M. C. Wang, & H. J. Walberg. *The effects of inclusion on learning.* Educational Leadership, 15(4), 33-35, 1994,1995.

Individuals with Disabilities Education Act (IDEA), PL 101-476, 1990.

Johnson, D. W., G. Maruyama, R. Johnson, D. Nelson, & L. Skon. *Effects of cooperative, competitive and individualistic goal structures on achievement: a meta-analysis.* Psychological Bulletin, 1981, 89, 47-62.

Johnson, D. W. & R. T. Johnson. *Cooperation and Competition: Theory and Research.* Edina, MN: Interaction Book Company, 1989.

Lipsky, D. K., & A.Gartner (Eds.) *Beyond Separate Education: Quality Education for All.* Baltimore, MD: Paul H. Brookes Publishing Co., 1989.

Meyer, L. H., & J. W. Putnam. *Social Integration. In V. B. Van Hasselt, P. S. Strain, & M. Hersen (Eds.), Handbook of development and physical disabilities.* Elmsford, NY: Pergamon, 1988.

National Center on Educational Restructuring and Inclusion (NCERI). *National Study of Inclusive Education.* Second Edition. New York, NY: The Graduate School and University Center, 1995.

Slavin, R. E. *Cooperative Learning: Theory, Research, and Practice.* Upper Saddle River, NJ: Prentice Hall, 1990.

Slavin, R. E. *Cooperative Learning: Theory, Research, and Practice. Second Edition.* Needham Heights, MA: Allyn & Bacon, 1995.

Weiner, R. *PL 94-142: Impact on the schools.* Washington, DC: Capitol Publications, 1985.

Reaching the Standards:

Second Language Learners

The history of the United States is marked by immigration. Since the 1930s, immigration into the U.S. has been steadily increasing. Unlike the past, when many immigrants were from English-speaking countries (predominantly from Europe and Canada), the majority of immigration into the U.S. now is from non-English-speaking countries. Today, in schools across the country, general education classrooms have many students whose first language is not English. Many of these students are faced with the dual challenge of becoming proficient in the English language and also meeting rising academic standards.

The current linguistic diversity of our nation's student population poses a formidable challenge for teachers. Many teachers have classrooms in which students have many different primary languages and many different levels of English proficiency. With the current focus on standards, an important question becomes: How do we best help students reach the standards while they are simultaneously learning English as a second language? How do we provide our language minority students with equal educational opportunity? In this chapter, we review language acquisition theory and the promise of cooperative learning for creating academic and linguistic success.

First, we briefly explore the Natural Order Hypothesis, a hypothesis outlining the natural stages of language acquisition. Next, we discuss the use of cooperative structures with language learners and offer some practical advice. We then examine why cooperative learning is so effective for language gains by exploring numerous prevailing theories and hypotheses about how students acquire a second language and how cooperative learning positively impacts input, output, interaction, and affective variables — all critical variables for becoming proficient in English.

Natural Order Hypothesis

The Natural Order Hypothesis postulates that as students learn a second language, they pass through five stages or levels: pre-production, early production, speech emergence, intermediate fluency, and finally fluency (Krashen & Terrell, 1983). In a typical classroom there are students at several stages of language acquisi-

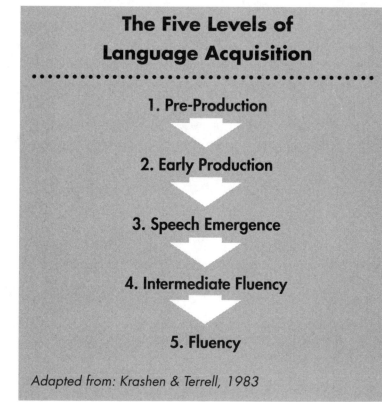

The Five Levels of Language Acquisition

1. Pre-Production

2. Early Production

3. Speech Emergence

4. Intermediate Fluency

5. Fluency

Adapted from: Krashen & Terrell, 1983

tion. Even a group of students who arrive in the country and begin school on the same day will have acquired vastly different capabilities in the target language within a few weeks.

Level 1: **Pre-Production**
The pre-production level describes students that are recent arrivals and are in their "Silent Period." The duration of this receptive phase of language development can be diminished through the comprehensible input and positive feelings of acceptance provided by cooperative teammates. During this phase it is important to keep in mind:
- Students are not expected to speak, read, or write.
- Before their ability to verbalize develops, students may understand what is said and be able to point, gesture, draw, sort, use manipulatives, or otherwise indicate understanding through nonverbal activities.
- When available, bilingual buddies can make classroom activities comprehensible in the primary language.

Level 2: **Early Production**
Students at this level have acquired enough oral language comprehension and confidence to begin to use single words. The may make errors in pronunciation and word choice that will be corrected through modeling by the teacher and cooperative teammates.

Level 3: **Speech Emergence**
At this level students are using words and phrases. Identify and post gambits for students to use for specific activities.

Level 4: **Intermediate Fluency**
This is the longest phase of the language acquisition process. Students master grammatical constructs and develop their social and academic vocabularies. Although students at this level are not reading and writing at grade level, their oral language may approximate native speakers.

Level 5: **Fluency**
Students achieve linguistic fluency.

Cooperative Structures and Language Learning
Cooperative learning structures can be adapted to accommodate language learners at all stages. In the structures presented in Chapter 8, suggested language acquisition adaptations are provided with each structure. Adaptations are provided for the different levels of language acquisition, where appropriate. When using the cooperative structures in this Teacher's Guide and video series to reach the standards with diverse language populations, consider the special adaptations.

One of the most important tools for success for limited English proficient students is the careful orchestration of types of cooperative learning teams. We strongly recommend, when possible, the use of two distinct types of teams: the homogeneous language team and the heterogeneous language team. The theory behind the use of these two types of teams is spelled out in Kagan, 1994; and the video *We Can Talk* (Kagan, 1993). We recommend homogeneous language teams

Language Tips

For all language acquisition stages it is important to support students with various contextual clues that make vocabulary and concepts comprehensible:

- **Use realia, pictures, and/or photographs when introducing new vocabulary.**

- **Design lessons that emphasize a variety of learning styles and multiple intelligences.**

- **Post word banks of new vocabulary.**

- **Monitor your speech rate and diction.**

- **Use authentic, natural speech.**

- **Limit direct instruction to no more than ten minutes.**

- **Check for understanding often.**

- **Involve students in cooperative interaction as part of every lesson.**

for content acquisition, and heterogeneous teams for language acquisition. The rationale for this recommendation is based on structuring to reach two distinct goals for early language learners: acquisition of the English language and acquisition of the academic content. When an early language learner learns difficult, abstract content in an unfamiliar language, the likely outcomes include little if any language learning and little if any content acquisition. If, on the other hand, the language learner learns new terms for familiar content, language learning is assured. And if the language learner learns new content in a language in which he/she is fluent, the probability of content acquisition is maximized. Thus, we recommend very different types of teams for mastering content and language.

When difficult, complex, abstract, or new content is introduced, we do not want language to be a barrier to the content. We recommend extensive use of the language that provides the greatest access to the content — often the primary language of students with limited English proficiency. Thus, when introducing content for which English might be a barrier, homogeneous language teams are used. That is, students are encouraged to break into pairs, triads, or teams of four with those most similar in language level. Some students may be working entirely in, say, Spanish, while others in sheltered English, and others yet in fluent English. Language level support materials are provided to teams to the extent possible including realia, text, cross-age tutors, and bilingual adult parents, volunteers, and classroom aides.

Once the content is mastered, it is important that students acquire the English language terms for the content. At that point, students return to their heterogeneous teams, each of which consists of a range of language levels. When a cooperative learning team mixes students at various stages of language acquisition, modeling and reinforcement of new language forms are frequent. Since language acquisition is a process, students continuously grow in acquisition of the target language when exposed to and interacting with a range of language levels. If there is a monolingual English-speaking student and a monolingual Spanish speaking student on the same team, ideally a bilingual student is placed on that team. Obviously, in forming heterogeneous language teams, we avoid teams consisting of monolingual students of different languages unless we can assign to that team bilingual students who can help negotiate meaning.

To maximize success in both the language and academic content, it is helpful to first introduce the content in a comfortable language and language level, but then provide activities in which the student must converse about and interact with the content using English. We do not try to stretch language level while dealing with unfamiliar content and we do not try to stretch content level using an unfamiliar language. Although the use of heterogeneous teams for language learning and homogeneous teams for content acquisition takes more set-up and transition time, it avoids the common, disastrous consequences of placing early language learners in a situation in which they attempt to obtain difficult, unfamiliar content in a difficult, unfamiliar language. By separating these two types of learning, we structure for success.

In cooperative learning activities that are appropriate for the class in general, but that require language production at a level above a particular student, that student can benefit from being a "buddy" to another student who will model output and provide comprehensible input in a more meaningful context.

It is important to keep in mind that although early language learners have a limited ability to respond orally and in writing, they do not necessarily have any limitations on their cognitive abilities. Use higher level questions that accommodate responses from students at all language acquisition stages.

Input
The Input Hypothesis

One of the most highly regarded and publicized hypotheses relating to language acquisition is the Input Hypothesis (Krashen, 1994). With regard to learning English as a second language, it is hypothesized that the student acquires English by understanding input that contains structures a little beyond the student's existing language proficiency. The hypothesis is symbolized as $i + 1$. This means input (i) that is at the student's current level of comprehension, plus language that is a bit beyond the student's level $(+ 1)$, helps the student acquire the next level of input. With a great volume of "comprehensible input" the student comes to understand the next level of language by using his/her current understanding and other cues such as the context and background knowledge.

According to the hypothesis, the language that students receive as input does not need to be "grammatically sequenced." That is, the input should not be explicitly targeted at the $i + 1$ formula. Deliberately sequencing

Benefits of Cooperative Learning on Language Input

• **More Input and More Complex Input**

• **More Active Listening**

• **More Comprehensible Input**

• **More Contextual Input**

• **More Genuine and Motivating Input**

• **More Naturally Varied Input**

• **More Redundant Input**

the language to the student's level of understanding may even be detrimental to acquisition. If the language the student is receiving is comprehensible to him or her, and there is enough of it, the i + 1 is automatically provided. This hypothesis is in contrast to the popular skill-building approach in which students learn rules, often through drills and exercises, then apply what they learn as they practice using the language.

Cooperative Learning and Input

The primary implication of the Input Hypothesis for the classroom is that in order for students to develop proficiency, they need to receive a great deal of comprehensible input. Cooperative learning creates a

language-rich classroom environment in which students have access to a great deal of input. Cooperative learning enhances English learning by providing more input, more complex input, more active listening, more comprehensible input, more contextual input, and naturally varied and redundant input. Although peer input in cooperative learning classrooms is potentially less accurate than teacher input, the benefits far outweigh its disadvantages.

More Input and More Complex Input

According to McGroarty (1993), research suggests that one of the main advantages of cooperative learning for language minority students is that the students have the opportunity to receive more input and at more complex cognitive levels. Limited English students in traditional classrooms receive less teacher and peer input and input at lower linguistic and cognitive levels (Arthur, et al., 1980; Schinke-Llano, 1983). In many traditional classrooms, the teacher provides the majority of the language input, then students are set to work independently. In the cooperative classroom, the language input does not cease. If the teacher is not producing language, teammates are.

While working closely with other students, students receive not only more input, but also more complex language. Through discussions and other cooperative interactions, students receive input beyond their level of proficiency. This increased complexity facilitates language development (Long & Porter, 1985; Pica, 1987). Studies in classrooms in which English is the primary language (Johnson & Johnson, 1983) show that cooperative learning compared with individual study in traditional classrooms provides more verbal input at each level: low (repetition), intermediate (stating new information), and high (explanations and integrations of information). Although the effects were not measured on second language learners, it is hypothesized that ESL students would similarly benefit from this increase in verbal input across the cognitive levels. Cooperative settings provide a natural medium for language acquisition because they are buzzing with language.

More Active Listening

Cooperative learning promotes more active listening than the whole-class structure. In the whole-class structure, input comes primarily from the teacher. Students may easily tune out, especially when the content is not motivating and no short-term individual accountability mechanisms are in place. In cooperative learning, students are more active participants than passive recipients. It is posited that students focus more on the input they receive in a more intimate setting, especially when comprehension is essential to contribute to the team's task, even if participation does not require language production.

More Comprehensible Input and More Contextual Input

Students working in teams have the luxury of tailoring their language to make it more comprehensible to the members for their team. To accomplish team tasks, teammates must understand each other. Teachers, because they are speaking to the entire class, cannot fine-tune their language to the different levels of language (Freeman & Freeman, 1994).

Contextual cues are crucial for students to understand input. Sheer language input outside of the ESL student's developmental level will be incomprehensible without cues to help the student make connections between the language and a concrete reality which the language is symbolizing. Aware of the importance of contextual cues, teachers successful with ESL students integrate more contextual cues into their teaching to provide students with more windows for comprehending the teacher input. Cooperative learning activities provide more contextual cues for an individual student than a teacher working with the entire class. Further, in cooperative teams the cues adding context and improving comprehension can be tailored more to an ESL teammate. If students see their teammate is not understanding them, they can use "Body English" to communicate or can provide a visual model of what's to be done.

The theory of multiple intelligences sheds light on the importance of contextual cues for language learners. One of the criteria for an intelligence in MI theory is the susceptibility to encoding in a symbol system (Gardner, 1983). Language is the symbol system for the verbal/linguistic intelligence. But ESL students cannot necessarily comprehend this symbol system and some prefer to tune into other stimuli, most notably visual and kinesthetic cues. Students acquire the language symbol system via other comprehensible symbol systems. In addition to students' ability to customize contextual cues to help ESL students understand, many cooperative learning strategies are multimodal. By virtue of their very design, they integrate language with visual and kinesthetic cues (for example, see Kagan & Kagan, 1998 for a range of cooperative learning and multiple intelligences strategies that engage the range of intelligences).

More Genuine and Motivating Input

An important aspect of the Input Hypothesis, according to Krashen (1983), is input that it is "genuinely interesting." Comprehensible input if not attended to by the learner is less likely to be acquired. Random language input is not nearly as effective in language development as is personally relevant, motivating input. Cooperative learning is rich in intrinsically motivating learning tasks. Further, since cooperative behavior is often instrumental in achieving team success, it often includes a motivating social reward system because teammates celebrate their successes. Many structures also have social skill components built in. The notions of more genuine and motivating learning tasks are supported by research that consistently finds students in cooperative learning spend more time on task compared with students in other learning situations (Kagan, 1994).

Naturally Varied and Redundant Input

Cooperative learning provides a natural setting for varied and redundant input. As students in small groups discuss a topic, they use a variety of phrases, providing the opportunity for the listener to triangulate in on meaning as well as receive the repeated input necessary for learning to move from short-term comprehension to long-term acquisition. Paraphrasing is built into many cooperative structures which provides redundant input, and often includes restating the same ideas in another way,

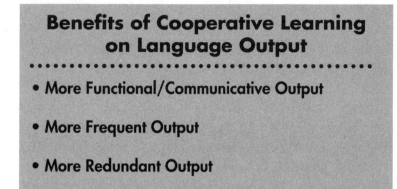

Benefits of Cooperative Learning on Language Output

• **More Functional/Communicative Output**

• **More Frequent Output**

• **More Redundant Output**

• **More Identity-Congruent Output**

giving the second language learner another opportunity to hear and understand what is being communicated. Additionally, paraphrasing promotes active listening. In turn-taking structures, students often state and restate the same ideas in many different ways, again providing variety and redundancy. Repetition and rephrasing improves comprehension.

The Issue of Accurate Input

A concern relating to the use of cooperative learning for students learning English is the notion of accurate input. In the traditional classroom, the teacher is the primary source of input for second language learners. Teachers may ensure that the language is accurate; teacher language may be grammatically correct with proper word choice and pronunciation. The language of peers is often less accurate than that of the teacher. Peers often use a conversational language rather than academic language. Non-native English speakers not yet fluent use "interlanguage." Interlanguage is an approximation of the target language. It could be argued, however, that conversational and interlanguage is more comprehensible for second language learners. Despite the possibility of reduced accuracy, peer output is a powerful positive source of language input for the language learner:

> Our experience is that interlanguage does a great deal more good than harm, as long as it is not the only input the students are exposed to. It is comprehensible, it is communicative, and in many cases, for many students it contains examples of i + 1. (Krashen & Terrell, 1983)

Output

Another theory relating to language proficiency is the Output Hypothesis. Output is the student's production of language through speech and writing. There are variations in the hypothesis, but the general proposition is that language proficiency is increased with increased output and with feedback on the comprehensibility of the student's production of language. This hypothesis has come under recent attack by Krashen (1994). Krashen argues that "only the Input Hypothesis is successful in accounting for the data in language acquisition and in the development of literacy." However, there are a number of benefits of language production when viewed through the filter of the Input Hypothesis: 1) output increases teacher input, 2) output encourages input from peers, 3) output increases students' confidence in language production, and 4) output provides meaningful input as students discuss their ideas, feelings, and thoughts (Jacobs, in press). Further, it is argued that language acquisition is fostered by output that is functional and communicative, frequent, redundant, and consistent with the identity of the speaker (Kagan,

1995). Cooperative learning provides a setting that promotes this type of output.

More Functional/Communicative Output

If speech is not representative of the way a speaker will use the language in everyday settings, it will add little to the speaker's actual communicative competence. Memorization of vocabulary lists or verb conjugations does not increase fluency because learning about a language is quite different from acquiring the language. Display behavior such as, "The clock is on the wall" or "This is a glass" is not representative of actual speech, and practice of this formal, decontextualized speech creates transference problems that hinder acquisition. The cooperative group provides the arena for expressive, functional, personally relevant, representative language output that is critical for language acquisition.

More Frequent Output

Students to a large extent learn to speak by speaking. A great advantage of cooperative learning over traditional classroom organization for the acquisition of language is the amount of language output allowed per student. Research in second language classrooms indicates language production is increased in student groups (Doughty & Pica, 1986). In the traditional classroom, students are called upon one at a time. During this whole-class, question-answer time, the teacher actually does more talking than the students because the teacher must talk twice for each time a student talks, first asking the question and then providing feedback in the form of praise, comment, or correction. Thus, in a classroom of 30 students, allowing each student one minute of output opportunity takes over an hour.

If, however, the students are in pairs, discussion takes a little over two minutes. Thus, a cooperative setting allows us to accomplish as much in two minutes as would be accomplished in an hour in a traditional classroom!

More Redundant Output

Students become fluent if they have the opportunity to speak repeatedly on the same topic. Many cooperative learning structures such as Three-Pair-Share and Inside/Outside Circle are explicitly designed to provide redundancy of output opportunities. Even informal, cooperative learning discussion provides redundancy as students discuss a topic with each of their teammates. There is not enough time in the traditional classroom to call on each student to talk more than once on a topic.

More Identity-Congruent Output

Practicing classroom speech that is not consistent with a student's identity will not lead to later fluency because the student will not want to project the identity associated with that speech. Cultural groups will resist acquisition of the dominant language if the very use of that language signals assimilation that is being resisted. Compared with the formal use of language practiced in whole-class settings, less formal, peer-oriented, expressive use of language in the cooperative group represents language use closer to the identity of many students. This more identity-congruent language facilitates language acquisition.

Interaction

The Interaction Hypothesis states that language is mastered through interaction with others. This hypothesis can be viewed as the combination of the Input and Output Hypotheses because true interactions between individuals require both input and output. The Interaction Hypothesis emphasizes the importance of social interactions for language development. McGroarty (1993) describes this view of language acquisition:

> Full mastery of language grows from interactions in the language that accomplish real-life ends; without experience in using the language to communicate information, accomplish tasks, express feelings, and play, learners will not grow in language competence.

This hypothesis aligns well with a functional perspective of language learning. Language is a social construct. Language evolved in our attempts to communicate with others. First language is fully acquired in social settings. And the meaning of language is negotiated within a social network. It is through meaningful interactions with others that language proficiency is best developed.

The implications for this basic hypothesis for the classroom are clear. If we wish to foster fluency in English, we must provide students the opportunities to interact in a meaningful way. Cooperative learning provides a context in which meaningful interactions are maximized. Cooperative learning improves the quality of interaction in a number of ways, including more negotiated meaning, more developmentally appropriate language, increased practice, questions, and a greater range of contexts.

Benefits of Cooperative Learning on Interaction Variables

• More Negotiated Meaning

• More Developmentally Appropriate Language

• More Practice Opportunities

• More Real Questions

• More Varied Group Settings

More Negotiated Meaning

Negotiation is a powerful element of student interactions that plays a key role in language acquisition (McGroarty, 1993; Kagan & McGroarty, 1993). As mentioned, language is a social construct and its meaning is largely shaped through interactions with others. Cooperative learning provides an arena in which students may negotiate the meaning of the language in context-based tasks. As students work together to accomplish their shared goals, they must communicate effectively. Students make input and output comprehensible as they discuss, direct and receive directions, ask and answer questions, and relate language to the task at hand and to their personal life experiences. Even in situations where language skills are limited, meaning may be derived through a process of negotiations.

More Developmentally Appropriate Language

A concept applicable to the development of language proficiency is Vygotsky's "Zone of Proximal Development." The growth of knowledge takes place in a social setting in which the learner, through interaction with another individual, receives information in an area just a little in advance of the learner's independent capabilities. This concept is very similar to the i + 1 of the Input Hypothesis. The difference is that the i + 1 is limited to input that is slightly beyond comprehensible input. In the interactionist perspective, it is the interaction that provides advanced input and output that stimulates the next step in language acquisition. The nature of a cooperative group focuses language in the Zone of Proximal Development. Through interactions with a partner or with teammates, students receive the scaffolding they need to stimulate language development to the next stage.

More Practice Opportunities

In the teacher-fronted classroom, students have very few opportunities to express themselves. Observations indicate that in the traditional classroom, 60 to 70 percent of the speech is generated by the teacher (Dunkin & Biddle, 1974; Goodlad, 1984; Pica & Doughty, 1985a, 1985b). This leaves the remaining 30 to 40 percent of the time to be divided among the students who participate in a sequential fashion. So, in an hour, each student gets approximately one minute to speak. In the cooperative learning classroom, this same quantity of language production can be accomplished in two minutes of pair discussion and in four minutes of team discussion (with students in teams of four).

In addition to the increased opportunities for practice, the language in a cooperative learning setting is more interactive. As students speak, they clarify meanings, paraphrase, ask for explanations, summarize, and discuss points of view. A review of research shows that cooperative learning in pair and group settings always increased opportunities to practice language, often resulted in improved oral skills, and added variety to the classroom activity (Gaies, 1985).

More Real Questions

Questions are an important variable that promote linguistic and cognitive development. Questions, by virtue of their nature, are an interactive process between the questioner and the answerer. They direct comprehensible input as well as provide students the opportunity to practice meaningful communication. In the typical traditional classroom, students ask one question per month on average (Sadker & Sadker, 1982). In cooperative learning, the opportunities for student-generated questions increases many times. Students in cooperative groups ask significantly more questions, and more varied questions, than in teacher-led classtime. Additionally, the questions in cooperative learning settings are real questions seeking truly wanted information as opposed to the frequently asked "display" questions teachers ask students (e.g., "What color is the book I am holding?"). Real questions stimulate subsequent discussion and elaboration, functional expansions that promote language acquisition.

More Varied Group Settings

Another linguistic benefit of cooperative learning is the increased variety of settings it provides students for language exchanges. In learning language through socialization, many different types of interactions are essential for developing the range of language proficiencies. Cooperative learning maximizes students' opportunities to interact in varied settings. A variety of cooperative learning structures adds variety to the settings in which students interact. In a Timed Pair Share and many other paired structures, students interact with one partner on their team; often students pair with different teammates for different interactions. In a RoundRobin and other team structures, students receive input from each teammate in turn and practice producing language; students often switch teams for different activities. In classbuilding structures such as Mix-Pair-Discuss, students interact with a different classmate with each round of discussion. Some structures (Team Interview, Three-Step Interview) emphasize question asking. Others (Choral Practice) emphasize practice of language. Yet others (Team

Benefits of Cooperative Learning on Affective Variables

• **Lower Anxiety**

• **More Cooperative Classroom Orientation**

• **More Peer Support**

• **Increased Self-Esteem**

• **Increased Motivation**

Statements) emphasize negotiation of meaning and consensus seeking. It is in these varied settings — entirely unavailable without the use of student-to-student cooperative interactions — that students learn to master a wide range of socially appropriate language skills.

Affective Variables
The Affective Filter

An important variable in the acquisition of language is the "affective filter." Negative affective variables such as high anxiety, low motivation, and low self-esteem hinder language acquisition. As Krashen (1994) indicates, these affective variables do not impact language acquisition directly, but rather they prevent input from reaching the acquisition device. The affective variables serve as a filter. If the filter is up, it creates a block and the student keeps the input out. As a result acquisition is hindered.

Cooperative Learning Lowers the Affective Filter

In addition to providing an environment which promotes language acquisition through input, output, and interaction, cooperative learning serves to lower the affective filter in a variety of ways, thus enabling students' language skills to emerge.

Lower Anxiety

Anxiety is a key variable that raises the affective filter and limits language learning. Krashen (1985) drives home the impact of anxiety on language learning:

> While not everything that is enjoyable is good for you, it may be the case that activities that are good for language acquisition are not anxiety-provoking, and those that are painful are not effective. It is possible that "no pain, no gain" does not apply to language acquisition.

The affective filter notion aligns well with the brain-based learning findings on what is commonly known as the "relaxed state of alertness." Jensen (1996) reviews research that discusses "good stress" and "bad stress." Stress can work to enhance performance when students feel challenged and feel they have the capacity to succeed. When students feel they can't succeed and are being forced to participate, learning and memory may be impaired.

The implications of this research for second language learners is that detrimental anxiety should be avoided. In a whole-class setting, the forced production of language in front of the classroom provokes anxiety because it poses a threat and may be perceived as a source of embarrassment and loss of prestige. Public error-correction also poses a threat. These unpleasant experiences are found to be ineffective at producing language gains (Horwitz et al., 1986; Young, 1990).

In the cooperative learning classroom, students work in small groups. Students who would be uncomfortable speaking in a public setting feel more comfortable producing language in a more intimate pair or team setting. The goal is to establish an optimum state of challenge for students. Students should not be forced to produce language beyond their capabilities. Many cooperative learning structures require language production. A highly recommended adaptation for second language students is that they are invited to participate orally, but have the opportunity to decline if they feel it is beyond their level of proficiency.

More Cooperative Classroom Orientation

The traditional classroom structure is a competitive structure where students compete for grades and attention. It has been argued (Kagan, 1985) that there is a mismatch between these classroom structures and the cooperative orientation of many linguistic and cultural minority students. This cultural bias helps explain the often-reported lower academic achievement of minority students. Students with a cooperative orientation often lack the motivation to achieve in culturally inappropriate environments in which the dominant focus is on competition and individual achievement. Further, competitive classroom structures increase anxiety and lead students who cannot compete on an equal-status footing to withdraw from the system. Alienation and failure deal a fatal blow to many students' delicate self-esteem.

Cooperative learning transforms the classroom orientation into a cooperative environment in which the goal is success for all students. Research finds that the greatest achievement gains in the cooperative classroom are for minority students (Kagan, 1985). A caring, cooperative classroom is an environment in which there is peer support and lower anxiety, which leads to increased self-esteem and motivation.

More Peer Support

One central principle common to most forms of cooperative learning is positive interdependence. Positive interdependence exists when students are all on the same side. It is created in a number of ways: through shared goals, rewards based on a cooperative performance, shared resources or roles, and tasks structured so students need the help of teammates to succeed. When positive interdependence is established, there is an increase in helping behaviors, peer tutoring, and checking for understanding. In many cooperative structures, praise and encouragement are built into the task. Students work together cooperatively because their success is positively correlated with the success of a teammate.

According to Glasser (1992), a sense of belonging is one of the most essential psychological needs. Cooperative learning fills the longing to belong, to fit in, to have a part to play. Students become a member of a team where they and their contribution are valued and appreciated. Teammates come to see each other as resources rather than obstacles, and as friends rather than competitors. Often in the cooperative classroom there are superordinate class goals so students identify themselves as members of the class, not only as members of the team. In the cooperative classroom, peer support is increased and the affective filter is lowered.

Increased Self-Esteem and Motivation

Competitive classroom structures create winners and losers. The winners are those who succeed academically, and the losers are those who don't. The potential to lose or fail releases two powerful forces: avoidance of failure and learned helplessness. Because of their fear of failing in a system for which they are linguistically ill-equipped, some students will simply choose not to participate. In an ego-preserving attempt, students opt not to participate. Students who make the effort to participate and repeatedly fail in the competitive environment soon learn that their efforts do not make a difference. They learn helplessness. Because they feel they have no control over the circumstances, they too choose not to participate. Avoidance of failure and learned helplessness have negative effects on self-concept and motivation. Students with high levels of self-esteem and motivation are more willing to attempt speaking in a difficult new language.

Affiliation is a central component to a positive self-concept (Borba, 1989). Teambuilding and classbuilding, frequent activities in the cooperative classroom, promote affiliation with teammates and classmates. Not surprisingly, research on cooperative learning finds improved self-esteem. Self-esteem fosters improved achievement and vice versa.

Cooperative learning meshes well with language acquisition theory. It provides rich and varied input — input containing language forms and content just a bit beyond the level of the language learner, maximizing the probability that the learner will take the next step in language acquisition. Language in cooperative learning conforms to all of the most important characteristics that enhance the probability of language learning: it is redundant, varied, genuine, and motivating. Perhaps most importantly, the language is received in a comprehensible context, rich with contextual cues which make

meaning far more probable. The speaker has the luxury of adjusting output to the level of the listener, a luxury not afforded the teacher speaking to a whole class of learners, each at a different stage of language acquisition.

Concluding Remarks

Cooperative learning also allows dramatically more language output and practice opportunities than does the traditional classroom. In the traditional class, we call most on those who least need the practice. Any naive observer would marvel at the absurdity of expecting language learning to spring from classrooms in which students seldom talk. But that is exactly what we do when we place early language learners in traditional classrooms. Consider, again, a traditional classroom with 30 students. If one person at a time talks, we use an entire hour to give each student two minutes of presentation time — and that only if the teacher doesn't say a word! Two minutes an hour will never add up. In fact the traditional structure is exquisitely designed to prevent language learning. In the cooperative format, language output is not only more frequent, but it is more genuine, communicative, and functional, and the language is used in a real-life context, a way which makes transfer from classroom experiences easy and probable.

As students in the cooperative classroom interact, they negotiate meaning and use language in developmentally appropriate ways. Peers pull language from their teammates as they interact: they motivate language use. Teammates communicate acceptance, lowering the affective filter. Early language learners who would not dare to raise their hands and speak before the whole class become quite fluent in the context of one or two other caring, supportive teammates.

We would not dream of teaching students to ride a bicycle by lecturing to them or having them read books about how to ride a bicycle. We learn the art of bicycle riding by riding. So too is it absurd to expect students to acquire the many skills of language fluency by lecturing at them or having them attempt only to read unfamiliar text. We learn to speak by speaking. Speaking in a safe, meaningful context in which it is OK to make mistakes as we negotiate meaning. That context is provided by cooperative learning which is carefully structured for the early language learner to maximize both content acquisition as well as language acquisition.

Resources

Arthur, B., R. Weiner, M. Culver, Y. J. Lee, & D. Thomas. *The Register of Impersonal Discourse to Foreigners: Verbal Adjustments to Foreign Accents.* In D. Larsen-Freeman (Ed.), *Discourse Analysis in Second Language Acquisition.* Rowley, MA: Newbury House, 1980.

Borba, Michele. *Esteem Builders: A Self-Esteem Curriculum for Improving Student Achievement, Behavior, and School/Home Climate.* Rolling Hills Estates, CA: Jalmar Press, 1989.

Doughty, C. & T. Pica. *Information gap tasks: Do they Facilitate Second Language Acquisition?* TESOL Quarterly 20(2), 305-326, 1986.

Dunkin, M. J., & B. J. Biddle. *The Study of Teaching.* New York, NY: Holt, Rinehart, & Winston, 1974.

Freeman, D. E. & Y. S. Freeman. *Between Worlds: Access to Second Language Acquisition.* Portsmouth, NH: Heinemann, 1994.

Gaies, S. J. *Peer Involvement in Language Learning.* Orlando, FL: Harcourt Brace Jovanovich, 1985.

Gardner, Howard. *Frames of Mind. The Theory of Multiple Intelligences.* New York, NY: Basic Books, 1983.

Glasser, William. *The Quality School: Managing Students Without Coercion.* New York, NY: Harper Collins, 1992.

Goodlad, John. *A Place Called School.* New York, NY: McGraw-Hill, 1984.

Horwitz, E., M. Horwitz, & J. Cope. *Foreign language classroom anxiety.* Modern Language Journal, 70, 125-132, 1986.

Jacobs, George. *Cooperative Learning and Second Language Teaching.* New York, NY: Cambridge University Press, In Press.

Jensen, Eric. *Brain-Based Learning.* Del Mar, CA: Turning Point Publishing, 1996.

Johnson, D. W. & R. T. Johnson. *Social Interdependence and Perceived Academic and Social Support in the Classroom.* Journal of Social Psychology, 120, 77-82, 1983.

Kagan, Spencer. *Cooperative Learning.* San Clemente, CA: Kagan Publishing, 1994.

Kagan, Spencer. *We Can Talk: Cooperative Learning for LEP Classrooms.* San Clemente, CA: Kagan Publishing, 1993.

Kagan, Spencer. *Dimensions of Cooperative Classroom Structures* in *Learning to Cooperate, Cooperating to Learn.* New York, NY: Plenum Press, 1985.

Kagan, Spencer. *We Can Talk: Cooperative Learning in the Elementary ESL Classrooms.* Elementary Education Newsletter 17(2), 3-4, 1995.

Kagan, S. & M. Kagan. *Multiple Intelligences: The Complete MI Book.* San Clemente, CA: Kagan Publishing, 1998.

Kagan, S. & M. McGroarty. *Principles of Cooperative Learning for Language and Content Gains.* In Holt, Daniel (Ed.). *Cooperative Learning: A Response to Linguistic and Cultural Diversity.* McHenry, IL: Delta Systems, Inc., 1993.

Krashen, S. & T. D. Terrell. *The Natural Approach: Language Acquisition in the Classroom.* Hayward, CA: Alemany, 1983.

Krashen, S. & T. D. Terrell. *The Input Hypothesis.* New York, NY: Longman, 1985.

Krashen, S. D. *The Input Hypothesis and Its Rivals.* In N.C. Ellis (Ed.), *Implicit and Explicit Learning of Languages.* San Diego, CA: Academic Press, 1994.

Long, M. H., & P. A. Porter. *Group Work, Interlanguage talk, and Second Language Acquisition.* TESOL Quarterly, 19, 207-228, 1985.

McGroarty, Mary. *Cooperative Learning and Second Language Acquisition.* In Holt, Daniel (Ed.). *Cooperative Learning: A Response to Linguistic and Cultural Diversity.* McHenry, IL: Delta Systems, Inc., 1993.

Pica, T., & C. Doughty *Input and Interaction in the Communicative Language Classroom: A Comparison of Teacher-fronted and Group Activities.* In S.M. Gass & C.G. Madden (Eds.), *Input in Second Language Acquisition.* Rowley, MA: Newbury House, 1985a.

Pica, T., & C. Doughty. *The role of group work in classroom second language acquisition.* Studies in Second Language Acquisition, 7, 233-248, 1985b.

Pica, T. *Second-Language Acquisition, Social Interaction and the Classroom.* Applied Linguistics, 8, 3-21, 1987.

Sadker, M., & D. Sadker. *Questioning Skills.* In *Classroom Teaching Skills, 2nd ed.* Lexington, MA: D. C. Heath & Co., 1982.

Schinke-Llano, L. A. *Foreigner Talk in Content Classrooms.* In H. W. Seliger & M. H. Long (Eds.), Classroom Oriented Research in Second Language Acquisition. Rowley, MA: Newbury House, 1983.

Young, D. *An investigation of students' perspectives on anxiety and speaking.* Foreign Language Annals, 23, 539-553, 1990.

chapter
SEVEN

Reaching the Standards Through

Multiple
Intelligences

Multiple

intelligences, Dr. Howard Gardner's theory of intelligence, provides insight into the minds of our students. It is truly a recognition and celebration of the diversity of human potential. Acknowledging that students possess different minds, learn differently, and display their knowledge in different ways holds tremendous potential for helping all students reach the standards.

If students differ in how they learn best, to maximize the potential learning for all students it is incumbent on us as teachers to use a range of instructional strategies. Multiple intelligences (MI) theory informs us both about the different ways students learn and about the different ways we must consequently teach if students are to reach the highest standards.

In this chapter we briefly overview the theory of multiple intelligences and the philosophy and methods of teaching which spring from it. We argue that success with the standards for all students cannot be achieved unless we adopt a range of teaching strategies aligned with the various ways students are smart. The Kagan Cooperative Learning Structures in this Teacher's Guide and video series represent one of our best hopes of aligning instruction with the range of intelligences to realize the maximum potential for all learners.

Brief Overview of Multiple Intelligences

In his influential book, *Frames of Mind* (1983), Dr. Howard Gardner put forth his theory of multiple intel-

ligences. Citing a wealth of evidence, Gardner made the case that there is not just one monolithic kind of intelligence. There is a whole spectrum of human intelligences. There are many ways to be smart. There are "multiple intelligences."

Gardner attempted to identify the key varieties of intelligences. He set forth some prerequisites that an intelligence must include and he tested candidate intelligences against specific criteria. The result was a list of seven intelligences. Gardner has since added the eighth intelligence, the Naturalist. See box: The Eight Intelligences.

The essence of these eight intelligences is attraction to and skill with different types of stimuli. Although all of

The Eight Intelligences

1. **Verbal/Linguistic**

2. **Logical/Mathematical**

3. **Visual/Spatial**

4. **Musical/Rhythmic**

5. **Bodily/Kinesthetic**

6. **Naturalist**

7. **Interpersonal**

8. **Intrapersonal**

us have all of the intelligences, we differ in their relative strength. For example, one student may be particularly strong in the verbal/linguistic and interpersonal/social intelligences. That student seeks, learns well from, and expresses him/herself well with words and in interpersonal relations. The student blossoms when taught with learning strategies which allow opportunity to interact with others and the opportunity to take in, process, and express him/herself with written and spoken language. In contrast, another student may not seek or be particularly skilled with words or people, but do wonderfully when taught with strategies which emphasize logical/mathematical relations and, say, music.

Human diversity is incredibly complex. Each of the eight intelligences has many facets. For example, one person may be strong in recognizing tunes (one facet of the musical/rhythmic intelligence) but quite weak in singing (a different facet of the musical/rhythmic intelligence). A person may do wonderfully well with inductive reasoning, but not at all well with abstract algebraic equations — two different facets of the logical/mathematical intelligence. Not only does each person have his/her own unique pattern of intelligences, each has a unique pattern of facets within each intelligence. An overview of the eight intelligences and the skills and preferences associated with each is presented at the end of this chapter.

Implications for Instruction

The greatest implication MI has for reaching the standards is the recognition that students learn in different ways. Dr. Gardner, in an interview for *Educational Leadership,* argues for a more differentiated approach to teaching students with multiple intelligences:

> What I argue against is the notion that there's only one way to learn to read, only one way to learn about biology. I think that such contentions are nonsense. (Checkley, 1997)

Gardner makes the case for teaching the existing disciplines in different ways. Since students are smart in many ways, there is not just one way to approach any subject matter. We can teach students to read, teach them the content and methods of biology, and every other discipline in a number of ways.

Dr. Thomas Armstrong, a leader in the field of MI, extends this perspective:

> MI theory suggests that no one set of teaching strategies will work best for all students at all times. All children have different proclivities in the seven intelligences, so any particular strategy is likely to be highly successful with one group of students and less successful with other groups. (Armstrong, 1994)

Anecdotal evidence supports this notion of a varied approach to teaching and learning. One of the most dramatic case studies in the multiple intelligences literature is the case history of Paula (Campbell, Campbell, & Dickinson, 1992). Early in school Paula was assessed as learning disabled; she developed very low self-esteem and a dislike for school. By fifth grade she was several grade levels behind her classmates. Paula attempted suicide in the summer before sixth grade. Her sixth grade teacher noticed Paula moved with poise and dignity. Following her hunch that Paula would benefit from kinesthetic instruction, Paula's teacher asked her to create a "movement alphabet" — movements to form the letters of the alphabet. Paula responded. Not only did she create letters, she sequenced them into a dance. Paula went on to dance her name, the words on the blackboard, spelling words, and even entire sentences. She performed for her class. Paula's self-esteem and liking for school increased, and by the end of sixth grade, Paula reached grade level in reading and writing. In seventh grade, she was mainstreamed in all classes and received above-average grades! The case of Paula demonstrates the potential of students to blossom when the instructional strategy matches their pattern of intelligences.

Research supports classroom success stories. In a case study of six schools implementing MI theory for five years or more, schools showed impressive achievement gains on standardized tests (Campbell & Campbell, 1999). The study included two elementary schools, two middle schools, and two high schools. In tests of basic skills, students outperformed their district, county, and national peers.

Two implications are particularly noteworthy. First, in the MI classroom, the focus is not teaching to the test, but rather creating engaging learning experiences that stimulate students' many ways of being smart. This supports the notion that teaching to the test, paradoxically, is not the most effective way to improve test scores. Educational approaches that create meaningful learning experiences and respect the uniqueness of the individual are promising. Students are well-served by a classroom that provides different pathways to success.

The second noteworthy implication of this research springs from the finding that the implementation of MI reduced or eliminated the disparity between the test scores of white and minority students. By adopting an approach that recognizes that all students have strengths and the ability to grow and learn, we make strides in helping all students reach high academic standards.

Three MI Visions

From multiple intelligences theory spring three visions for educators: Matching, Stretching, and Celebrating (see Kagan & Kagan, 1998). Each of the three visions is related to our ability as teachers to support all learners in reaching the standards.

Matching

Paula is a dramatic example of the power of matching. Paula had been taught year after year, to little avail. Why? She had been taught with instructional strategies which did not match the way she best learned. Then Paula had the good fortune to be assigned a sensitive teacher who recognized the need to teach Paula with a kinesthetic instructional strategy. In a few months Paula made up several years of academic deficit. Why? The way she was taught matched the way she was smart.

By matching the way we teach to the ways all students best learn, we provide access to the curriculum for all students. The goal in Matching is to maximize academic success in all the areas of the curriculum for all students. The goal is reached by using multiple intelligences instructional methods. Academic success is partially a function of the extent to which we match instruction

Vision 1: **Matching**

- Matching instructional strategies with students' intelligences
- Providing access to the curriculum for all students
- Building multiple bridges onto the curriculum
- Teaching the curriculum through all intelligences
- Creating windows for learning for all learners
- Teaching with MI

***The more ways we teach,
the more students we reach —
And the more ways we reach each!***

Adapted from: Kagan & Kagan, 1998

to students' multiple intelligences. All aspects of the curriculum are made more accessible when delivered through instructional strategies which match the intellectual strengths of each student.

It is important to note that this first vision calls for a shift not in curriculum, but in instruction. Paula's teacher did not question the importance of teaching her spelling words, she made a shift only in the method to get there — to teach with kinesthetic rather than traditional methods.

Theoretically, all we need do is teach with instructional strategies for each of the intelligences, thus making an otherwise inaccessible curriculum accessible and doing wonders to boost self-esteem and liking for school in

the process! In essence, we match the way we teach with the way students are smart. In Gardner's (1993) words:

> In this way, the student is given a secondary route to the solution to the problem, perhaps through the medium of an intelligence that is relatively strong for that individual.

It is not practical to expect a teacher to assess the unique pattern of intelligences of each student and to design unique instructional strategies for each student. This is not necessary. If a teacher uses a range of instructional strategies — strategies which engage the range of intelligences — all students will have access to the curriculum through their preferred intelligences. It is for that reason that we developed structures for each of the intelligences (Kagan & Kagan, 1998). The cooperative learning structures in this series engage a range of intelligences. (See Multiple Intelligences Chart of Structures.)

Stretching

The second MI vision is stretching — stretching all students to become as smart as they can in all facets of all of the intelligences. One of the great gifts of MI theory is to move us as a community of educators away from thinking of intelligence as a given, a limit. Old fashioned IQ-style thinking would have us believe that each person is born with a given IQ that changes little throughout life. MI thinking would have us realize that the more any facet of any intelligence is engaged, the more it develops. We can all be smarter in all of the intelligences!

Vision 2: **Stretching**

· ·

- Stretching students' multiple intelligences
- Nurturing the development of each intelligence
- Developing students' dominant and nondominant intelligences
- Fostering growth in all facets of all intelligences
- Enhancing students' capacities in each intelligence
- Teaching for MI

Helping students stretch every facet of every intelligence! Making students smarter in many ways!

Adapted from: Kagan & Kagan, 1998

Again, it is not practical to expect teachers to assess the unique pattern of intelligences of each student and to design special programs to develop each student's intelligences. Stretching can occur with no individualized programs. If a range of instructional strategies are used with all students — strategies which engage the range of intelligences — over time all intelligences will be engaged and stretched.

It is important to engage and stretch all intelligences among our students if we are to maximize their potential for reaching the standards. For example, as students develop their visual/spatial intelligence, they will perform better in geometry, geography, and even descriptive writing. As they develop their naturalist intelligence, they will perform at a higher level, not just in their

science courses, but in all other courses that require sensitivity to the natural world. As we develop the logical intelligence, it empowers students not just in reaching the mathematics standards, but also in designing an experiment with fewer plausible alternative hypotheses, writing a more logical essay, inducing and applying principles from history, and in using logic to more accurately answer any exam.

Celebrating

The third vision is celebrating. To the extent we realize this third vision, our students come to celebrate their own uniqueness and the diversity among them. Each student needs to know and accept his or her own unique pattern of intelligences. They need also to understand that each of us differs in our pattern of intelligences.

When we are engaged in old fashioned IQ-style thinking, there is but one yardstick to measure everyone and everyone in the world stacks up above some people and below others. Multiple intelligences theory breaks the yardstick by showing us there are many ways to be smart. We stop asking of others how smart they are and start asking how they are smart! In the process social encounters are transformed. Students move away from the competitive measures of each other in terms of "Who is up and who is down." Instead they begin to see others as resources, asking how they might work together to complement each other's strengths. Students realize that none of us is smartest in all intelligences and that our real strength lies in our diversity.

As students honor the unique pattern of intelligences in others, they obtain diversity skills which create an

Vision 3: Celebrating

- Understanding and celebrating our own unique pattern of intelligences
- Improving ourselves through metacognition and reflection
- Respecting others' unique pattern of intelligences
- Appreciating differences
- Celebrating our collective diversity
- Teaching about MI

Honoring uniqueness and celebrating diversity! Asking not how smart we are, but how we are smart!

Adapted from: Kagan & Kagan, 1998

accepting, supportive community. The feeling of being accepted, even celebrated, rather than put down for one's uniqueness is conducive to creating an inclusive learning environment. Early language learners and all learners attempting new and difficult content are willing to take risks and persist in the face of failure to the extent they feel accepted. If they feel fear of rejection, they downshift, operating at a lower cognitive level. We simply are not our best when we are anxious or afraid. If we want all students to blossom, to reach their fullest potential, we need to create accepting learning environments. One key to creating safe, supportive learning environments in which all students have maximum opportunity to reach the standards is to encourage students to celebrate their own uniqueness and the diversity of intelligences among us.

Realizing the Visions Through Kagan Structures

A major thrust of our work in cooperative learning has been and continues to be the development and training of cooperative learning structures. These cooperative structures are multimodal, step-by-step instructional strategies that integrate many intelligences. Some structures engage the verbal/linguistic intelligence, others the logical/mathematical intelligence, and yet others the visual/spatial intelligence. We have developed structures for each of the intelligences of multiple intelligences theory. The structures provide the most practical way to realize all three visions of MI theory.

When we teach with a full range of structures, we match our instruction to the full range of patterns of intelligences among our students. We provide access to the curriculum for all students. Further, because the structures engage the range of intelligences, they stretch each intelligence. Finally, each new way we teach provides new opportunities for students to understand, accept, and celebrate their own uniqueness and the diversity among them. A student who did poorly in a logical structure might become the leader of the group when a kinesthetic or musical structure is used. Teammates come to appreciate the unique talents of each person. Feeling accepted, students blossom and are more likely to realize their potential.

As we train teachers how and when to use the various cooperative learning structures, we use a toolbox analogy. The Kagan structures are tools in a teacher's toolbox. The more tools we have in our toolbox, the

Multiple Intelligences Chart of Structures

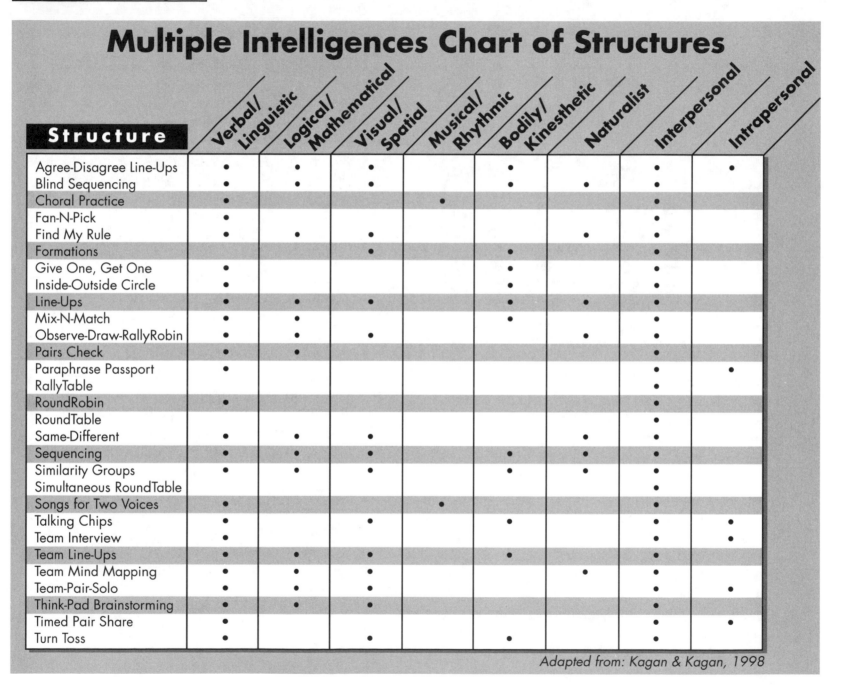

Structure	Verbal/ Linguistic	Logical/ Mathematical	Visual/ Spatial	Musical/ Rhythmic	Bodily/ Kinesthetic	Naturalist	Interpersonal	Intrapersonal
Agree-Disagree Line-Ups	•	•	•		•		•	•
Blind Sequencing	•	•	•		•	•	•	
Choral Practice	•			•			•	
Fan-N-Pick	•						•	
Find My Rule	•	•	•			•	•	
Formations			•		•		•	
Give One, Get One	•				•		•	
Inside-Outside Circle	•				•		•	
Line-Ups	•	•	•		•	•	•	
Mix-N-Match	•	•			•		•	
Observe-Draw-RallyRobin	•	•	•			•	•	
Pairs Check	•	•					•	
Paraphrase Passport	•						•	•
RallyTable							•	
RoundRobin	•						•	
RoundTable							•	
Same-Different	•	•	•			•	•	
Sequencing	•	•	•		•		•	
Similarity Groups	•	•	•		•	•	•	
Simultaneous RoundTable							•	
Songs for Two Voices	•			•			•	
Talking Chips	•		•		•		•	•
Team Interview	•						•	•
Team Line-Ups	•	•	•		•		•	
Team Mind Mapping	•	•	•			•	•	
Team-Pair-Solo	•	•	•				•	•
Think-Pad Brainstorming	•	•	•				•	
Timed Pair Share	•						•	•
Turn Toss	•		•		•		•	

Adapted from: Kagan & Kagan, 1998

SCIENCE Reaching the Standards Through Cooperative Learning
Kagan, Kagan & Kagan

more efficient we are in building meaningful learning experiences for our students. If we hired a carpenter to build us a house, but the carpenter knew how to only use a hammer, we would end up with a poor excuse for a house. The same would be true if the carpenter could use only a saw. But if the carpenter had a toolbox full of tools and could switch artfully among the hammer, the saw, and the wrench, we would be much more likely to end up with an interesting, luxurious, beautiful, and functional house. In a similar way, if we as teachers rely on but a few instructional strategies, we are less likely to build meaningful, engaging learning experiences for our students.

As teachers, the better equipped we are with a wide range of instructional strategies for each intelligence, the more likely we will reach students dominant in each intelligence. Each student has different proclivities in the various intelligences. Any single strategy may be very successful with some students, yet less successful with others. Using a range of teaching strategies makes learning more accessible to all students. Further, by using a range of structures, we are more likely to stretch students in all intelligences, and more likely to afford each student the opportunity to celebrate their own uniqueness and their collective diversity.

Thus the structures realize the visions.

And, as we have seen, to the extent we realize the three visions of multiple intelligences theory, we maximize the probability all students will reach the standards. To review:

Vision 1, Matching, helps us help all students reach the standards by matching the way we teach to the ways all students best learn. All aspects of the curriculum are made more accessible when delivered through instructional strategies which match the intellectual strengths of each student.

Vision 2, Stretching, helps us help all students reach the standards because a student's growth in one intelligence has implications for all academic areas. As we have seen, a stretch in logic does not predict success only in mathematics but also in science, social studies, and language arts.

Vision 3, Celebrating, helps us help all students reach the standards because all learners attempting new and difficult content are willing to take risks and persist in the face of failure to the extent they feel accepted. The alternative is fear of rejection and downshifting, which limits the probability that students will reach their potential. Only if students accept themselves and feel accepted by others can they optimize their potential in reaching the standards.

Because the cooperative learning structures in this Teacher's Guide and video series engage a range of intelligences, they help realize the visions. This in turn increases the probability of all students reaching the standards.

Verbal/Linguistic Intelligence

We use our verbal/linguistic intelligence to think in, with, and about words. Oral and written language are symbols to think in and express this intelligence. Those strong in the verbal/linguistic intelligence enjoy reading, writing, speaking, and listening. Some forms of this intelligence include telling jokes, discussing, writing poems, and passing notes.

Educational Implications

• **Matching:** Students strong in the verbal/linguistic intelligence learn best through listening to verbal presentations, reading, writing, and discussing. They benefit from audio tapes in the class listening bar. They enjoy structures such as Draw-What-I-Write, RoundTable, and Brainstorming.

• **Stretching:** We develop the verbal/linguistic intelligence as we have students create oral presentations, written essays, poems, debates, dialog journals, book reports, and summaries of lectures. The verbal/linguistic intelligence is stretched also as students learn foreign languages and hone traditional language arts skills such as vocabulary, syntax and grammar, and the various genres of writing. We may stretch students' linguistic intelligence through the other intelligences as when we have them write word problems, discuss their artwork, and share their goals.

• **Celebrating:** Students celebrate their word smarts through positive peer response groups, self-validation following oral and written presentations, writer's journals, and written entries in their portfolios.

Attracted To
• Words; Oral and Written Language

Skills & Preferences
• Communicating (oral and written)
• Creating stories
• Debating, discussing
• Learning foreign languages
• Playing word games
• Reading with comprehension
• Remembering quotes, sayings
• Spelling easily
• Telling jokes, puns, rhymes
• Using correct grammar
• Using rich vocabulary
• Writing (descriptive and humorous)

Adapted from: Kagan & Kagan, 1998

Logical/Mathematical Intelligence

We use our logical/mathematical intelligence to think in, with, and about numbers and relations. Numbers and symbols representing relations express this intelligence. Those strong in the logical/mathematical intelligence enjoy solving problems, quantifying outcomes, and determining relations such as cause-effect and if-then relations. Some forms of this intelligence include creating, thinking about, and solving problems; analyzing objects and situations for their components; using abstract symbols; and discovering and using algorithms and logical sequences.

Educational Implications

• **Matching:** Students strong in the logical/mathematical intelligence learn best through problems and opportunities to analyze. They benefit from asking questions, experimenting, and analyzing results in an attempt to solve problems and understand reality. They enjoy structures such as Find My Rule and Jigsaw Problem Solving.

• **Stretching:** We develop the logical/mathematical intelligence as we have students solve problems, perform experiments, learn and develop algorithms, make predictions, discover relationships, categorize information, and engage in inductive and deductive reasoning. Skills with patterns and functions, probability, statistics, measurement, and logic can be developed across the curriculum. We may stretch students' logical intelligence through the other intelligences as when we have them write the steps, graphically depict the sequence, and discuss the rationale.

• **Celebrating:** Students celebrate their number smarts by sharing and appreciating their different approaches to problem solving, analyzing their own progress in math and science, and including samples of their problem-solving skills in their portfolios.

Attracted To
• Numbers, Relations, Problems

Skills & Preferences
• Analyzing
• Computing
• Deducing
• Discovering functions, relations
• Estimating, predicting
• Experimenting
• Figuring things out
• Finding, creating patterns
• Inducing
• Organizing, outlining, sequencing
• Playing strategy games
• Questioning
• Reasoning abstractly
• Selecting, using algorithms
• Sequencing
• Solving logic problems
• Using abstract symbols

Adapted from: Kagan & Kagan, 1998

Visual/Spatial Intelligence

We use our visual/spatial intelligence to think in, with, and about visual images. We think in and express this intelligence through pictures, sculpture, arranging objects, and finding our way around. Those strong in the visual/ spatial intelligence enjoy doodling, designing, drawing, combining colors, and arranging objects, and they often have a good sense of direction. Some forms of this intelligence include map interpreting and making, decorating, and page layout.

Educational Implications

• **Matching:** Students strong in the visual/spatial intelligence learn best through visual input such as charts, graphs, models, drawings, photographs, computer animations, and films and videos. They benefit from opportunities to express themselves or create reports in visual formats and create icons to represent content. They enjoy structures such as Match Mine, Mind Mapping, and Guided Imagery.

• **Stretching:** We develop the visual/spatial intelligence as we have students create maps, diagrams, charts, two-dimensional and three-dimensional models, pictures, and videos. To develop this intelligence we explore elements of art including color, light and shading, lines and shapes, patterns and designs, texture, and various mediums. We may stretch students' spatial intelligence through the other intelligences as when we have them make rhythms corresponding to patterns, write about their art, and use nature as the subject.

• **Celebrating:** Students celebrate their picture smarts through posting and displaying visual products. They give and receive feedback to each other on their models and art projects. They celebrate also by drawing in their journals and selecting and commenting on drawings, videos, and other visual products they place in their portfolios.

Attracted To
• Spatial Relations, Shape, Size, Color

Skills & Preferences
• Appreciating, creating architecture
• Arranging, decorating
• Building models
• Charting, graphing
• Coordinating colors
• Creating, interpreting graphic organizers
• Creating designs, graphics, layouts
• Decorating, interior design
• Imagining in vivid detail, visualizing
• Navigating, sense of direction
• Painting, sketching, drawing
• Playing spatial games
• Reading, creating maps
• Remembering visual details
• Rotating figures mentally
• Sculpting, molding, designing
• Thinking in pictures and images

Adapted from: Kagan & Kagan, 1998

Musical/Rhythmic Intelligence

We use our musical/rhythmic intelligence to think in, with, and about music. Melodies and rhythms can be symbols to think in and express this intelligence. Those strong in the musical/rhythmic intelligence enjoy listening to and creating music in many forms. Some forms of this intelligence include playing instruments, singing songs, reading music, composing melodies and lyrics, and appreciating music.

Educational Implications

• **Matching:** Students strong in the musical/rhythmic intelligence learn and remember best through musical input such as songs, raps, and chants. They enjoy a classroom in which music is played in the background. They benefit from opportunities to express themselves musically through musical and rhythmic products. They enjoy structures such as Songs for Two Voices, Team Chants, and Lyrical Lessons.

• **Stretching:** We develop the musical/rhythmic intelligence as we have students sing, play, react to, analyze, and compose music. A wide range of musical genre stretches different facets of the intelligence so we include humming, singing, tapping, clapping, snapping, and playing a range of electronic, string, percussion, and wind instruments. A differentiated musical/rhythmic curriculum includes development of specific skills such as recognizing and producing pitches, rhythms, tempos, and timbre. We may stretch students' musical intelligence through the other intelligences as when we have them write lyrics, draw their reaction to a song, and discuss their interpretation.

• **Celebrating:** Students celebrate their music smarts through recitals of various types and adding musical/rhythmic entries into their portfolios.

Attracted To
• Rhythms, Melodies, Lyrics, Pitch, Timing, Timbre

Skills & Preferences
• Composing melodies, lyrics
• Humming, chanting, whistling
• Identifying instruments
• Keeping time, recognizing rhythm
• Learning through lyrics
• Listening to, appreciating music
• Playing by ear
• Playing instruments
• Reading and writing music
• Recognizing melodies, songs, composers
• Singing, rapping
• Singing with perfect pitch
• Tapping feet, hands
• Understanding structure of music

Adapted from: Kagan & Kagan, 1998

Bodily/Kinesthetic Intelligence

We use our bodily/kinesthetic intelligence to think in, with, and about movement and gestures. Facial and hand gestures and movements are symbols to think in and express this intelligence. Those strong in the bodily/ kinesthetic intelligence enjoy physical activities, hands-on activities, acting, and developing physical skills.

Educational Implications

• **Matching:** Students strong in the bodily/kinesthetic intelligence learn best through movement and hands-on activities. They learn well when there is movement to symbolize the content. They benefit from opportunities to express themselves or create reports which include acting, mime, or movement. They enjoy structures such as Kinesthetic Symbols, Formations, Folded Value Lines, and Agreement Circles.

• **Stretching:** We develop the bodily/kinesthetic intelligence as we have students communicate through body language, dance, develop fine and gross motor skills, and learn the art of various physical activities, sports, and performances. Speed, strength, flexibility, agility, coordination, and endurance are keys to stretching the bodily kinesthetic intelligence. We may stretch students' kinesthetic intelligence through the other intelligences as when we have them reflect on their acting, write about a physical activity, or interact with nature.

• **Celebrating:** We celebrate being body smart by keeping records of bodily/ kinesthetic accomplishments and progress: students move their names up the appropriate chart as they can juggle more items or in more ways, can do more pull-ups, or master another dance step. Live performances by teams and individuals offer opportunities to receive feedback and to celebrate. Students learn to accept winning with humility and accept losing with grace. Video recordings of dance and performances are possible portfolio entries.

Attracted To
• Movement, Body Language, Hands-on Activities, Athletics

Skills & Preferences
• Acting, mime
• Athletic performances
• Dancing, choreographing
• Exercising, working out
• Fine motor skills, hand-eye coordination
• Gross motor skills, endurance, strength
• Juggling
• Learning through "hands-on" activities
• Manipulating things
• Mimicking
• Moving with grace and coordination
• Playing sports
• Using gestures, body language

Adapted from: Kagan & Kagan, 1998

Naturalist Intelligence

We use our naturalist intelligence to think about plants, animals, clouds, rocks, and other natural phenomena. Those strong in the naturalist intelligence enjoy collecting, analyzing, studying, and caring for plants, animals, and environments. They are sensitive to interdependence within ecologies and to environmental issues.

Educational Implications

• **Matching:** Students strong in the naturalist intelligence learn best through presentations involving natural phenomena, by bringing natural phenomena into the classroom, and by having students interact with nature through field trips. They learn best when the content may be sorted and classified or related to the natural world through analogies. They enjoy structures such as Look-Write-Discuss, Same-Different, Observe-Write-RoundRobin, and Categorizing.

• **Stretching:** Students stretch their naturalist intelligence as they study flora and fauna, regions and habitats, weather and climate, rocks and minerals, and hone their observational and recording skills. We may stretch students' naturalist intelligence through the other intelligences as when we have them record or draw their observations in a log, develop classification systems, and learn about nature through music.

• **Celebrating:** Students celebrate their nature smarts through harvesting the fruits of their gardens, demonstrating their care for animals, and recording positive interactions with the environment such as steps to counter pollution. Portfolio contributions may include excerpts from their nature log.

Attracted To
• Plants, Animals, Natural Phenomena, the Environment

Skills & Preferences
• Appreciating plants, flowers, trees
• Caring for plants, gardens, pets, wild animals
• Classifying flora, fauna, natural phenomena
• Collecting plants, insects, rocks
• Discovering patterns in nature
• Enjoying animal antics
• Observing details
• Predicting the weather
• Protecting the environment
• Recognizing species, rocks, stars, clouds
• Taming, training animals
• Understanding environmental interdependence

Adapted from: Kagan & Kagan, 1998

Interpersonal Intelligence

We use our interpersonal intelligence to know and interact successfully with others. Those strong in the interpersonal intelligence enjoy working with, caring for, and learning with others. Some forms of this intelligence include leadership skills, friendship skills, and ability to understand points of view different from one's own.

Educational Implications

• **Matching:** Students strong in the interpersonal intelligence learn best through interacting with others about the content. They benefit from opportunities to interact with others with differing points of view. They enjoy structures such as Jigsaw, Telephone, Paraphrase Passport, Mix-Pair-Discuss, Team Interview, and Numbered Heads Together.

• **Stretching:** We develop the interpersonal intelligence as we have students debate, use cooperative learning, interview others, and do surveys. The interpersonal intelligence is stretched as students learn leadership skills, negotiation, peacemaking, empathy, role-taking, communication skills, respect, honesty, and teamwork skills. We may stretch students' interpersonal intelligence through the other intelligences as when we have them reflect on their interaction with others, build creative cooperative projects, explore nature together, and compose songs and sing together in harmony.

• **Celebrating:** Students celebrate their people smarts as they share what they have learned from and about others. They celebrate their increasing teamwork and leadership skills, and include pages from their peer dialog journals as entries in their portfolios.

Attracted To
• Other People, Interaction

Skills & Preferences
• Caring for, teaching others
• Communicating with others
• Interacting with others
• Empathizing and sympathizing with others
• Leading and organizing groups and events
• Making and maintaining friends
• Resolving conflicts, mediating
• Respecting rights, point of view of others
• Seeing things from another's perspective
• Showing sensitivity to the moods and motives of others
• Understanding thoughts, values, needs of others
• Working as team member

Adapted from: Kagan & Kagan, 1998

Intrapersonal Intelligence

We use our intrapersonal intelligence to think in, with, and about internal feelings, moods, and states of mind. Dream images and feelings are symbols to think in and express this intelligence. Those strong in the intrapersonal intelligence enjoy solitude, contemplation, and an opportunity to explore inner states and thoughts including preferences, plans, fantasies, memories, and feelings.

Educational Implications

• **Matching:** Students strong in the intrapersonal intelligence learn best through introspection, reflection, and individual think time. They benefit from alone time to write, draw, doodle, or allow their thoughts to incubate. They enjoy structures such as Journal Reflections, Timed-Pair-Share, Corners, and Think Time.

• **Stretching:** We develop the intrapersonal intelligence as we have students engage in metacognition and/or free association on their own behavior and feelings. The intrapersonal intelligence is stretched as students attempt to determine their own patterns of intelligences, examining their strengths and weaknesses, and exercising intrapersonal skills such as introspection, planning, metacognition, reflection, value clarification, prioritizing, self-discipline, and time management. We may stretch students' intrapersonal intelligence through the other intelligences as when we have them write journal reflections, relate problems to personal experience, and choreograph personally relevant movements.

• **Celebrating:** Students celebrate their self smarts through sharing interpretations of their dreams, analyzing internal strengths and weaknesses, setting and checking progress on self-determined goals, and weighing their own products to select those most representative of themselves as contributions to their portfolios.

Attracted To
• Internal experiences: Moods, Memories, Intuitions, Values, Feelings, Fantasies

Skills & Preferences
• Attending to memories, fantasies, dreams
• Clarifying own values and beliefs
• Controlling impulses
• Developing differentiated opinions, beliefs
• Enjoying think time, alone time, quiet time
• Introspecting, intuiting
• Knowing and managing moods and feelings
• Knowing own strengths and weaknesses
• Motivating oneself
• Setting realistic goals
• Thinking about one's own thinking
• Understanding inner conflicts, motivations

Adapted from: Kagan & Kagan, 1998

Resources

● ●

Armstrong, Thomas. *Multiple Intelligences in the Classroom.* Alexandria, VA: Association for Supervision and Curriculum Development, 1994.

Campbell, L., & B. Campbell. *Multiple Intelligences and Student Achievement: Success Stories from Six Schools.* Alexandria, VA: Association for Supervision and Curriculum Development, 1999.

Campbell, L., B. Campbell, & D. Dickinson. *Teaching and Learning Through Multiple Intelligences.* Needham Heights, MA: Allyn & Bacon, 1992.

Checkley, K. *The first seven...and the eighth: A conversation with Howard Gardner.* Educational Leadership, 1997, 55(1) 10.

Gardner, Howard. *Frames of Mind. The Theory of Multiple Intelligences.* New York, NY: Basic Books, 1983.

Kagan, S. & M. Kagan. *Multiple Intelligences: The Complete MI Book.* San Clemente, CA: Kagan Publishing, 1998.

Cooperative Learning Structures

The preceding chapters have focused on educational standards and the use of cooperative learning to help students in heterogeneous classrooms reach the standards. The challenge of providing for ALL learners in general education classrooms is diminished through the effective implementation of cooperative learning.

Through cooperative learning, we establish an inclusive classroom environment in which students with physical, cognitive, and behavioral or emotional disabilities are not only brought into regular classrooms, but are truly included in classroom learning activities. Structured interactions that integrate the basic principles of cooperative learning increase participation by all. Only when students are given equal status in the classroom, have access to the same curriculum, are expected to participate, and classroom activities are structured to maximize active participation for all students, do all students truly stand a chance of reaching high academic standards. Surely certain adaptations and modifications are essential for students with disabilities. Yet with support and effective teaching strategies, all students truly can be integrated into the classroom. And we can provide for all students without discrimination.

The same is true for students with limited English proficiency. In the cooperative learning classroom, students achieve linguistic fluency through increased social interaction, increased opportunities to receive comprehensible language input, and increased opportunities to produce language in meaningful context. Through the supportive atmosphere established by the use of cooperative learning, the affective filter is lowered and students have increased opportunities to reach the standards while building verbal fluency.

Multiple intelligences informs us that students possess different minds and learn differently. By matching the instruction to students' intelligences, we provide greater access to the curriculum. We offer our students more opportunities to reach the standards. Through the integration of visuals, music, movement, and productive social interaction — so natural to the multimodal structures of cooperative learning — we respect our students' individual differences and equalize their ability to reach the standards.

Indeed, cooperative learning, as an inclusive classroom orientation and as a set of specific classroom structures, is a powerful teaching and learning tool. Perhaps that is why cooperative learning has initiated more research investigations than any other educational intervention in history: the breadth and strength of the effects are unparalleled.

In this chapter, and in the accompanying video series, we endeavor to move beyond the research and theory. We provide the nuts and bolts of powerful cooperative learning structures and show how they can be used to effectively reach the standards.

The Kagan Structures

The structures in this chapter are presented in the order in which they appear on the video. For most structures, we provide 1) step-by-step instructions to make it easy to use in your classroom, 2) variations, 3) management hints, 4) a link to the structure featured in the video, 5) adaptations of the structure for special students, 6) activity ideas of how to use the structure to reach the standards, and 7) blackline masters.

Adaptations for Special Students
The special adaptations are for students with disabilities to facilitate inclusion and for ESL students to promote language acquisition.

Inclusion Adaptations
The adaptations for inclusion are provided according to the three categories of disabilities as described in Chapter 5:
- Physical Disabilities
- Cognitive Disabilities
- Behavioral or Emotional Disabilities

English as a Second Language (ESL)
Suggested adaptations for English second-language learners are provided for four stages of language learning as described in Chapter 6:
- Pre-Production
- Early Production
- Speech Emergence
- Intermediate Fluency

In the Video
Each structure presented includes an "In the Video" section. This section links the structure presented here to the structure demonstrated in the video. We describe how the structure is used to reach an educational objective relating to the content standards.

Reaching the Standards with Structures
For each structure presented, we provide various ideas and activities of how to use the structure to reach the standards. The ideas and activities provided here are not intended as a comprehensive curriculum. The structures in this Teacher's Guide are but a small subset of instructional strategies that we can use to effectively reach the standards. They are provided as a model of the structural approach: how to reach high academic standards for all students through structures.

Not every structure includes ideas for each standard because some structures are not well-suited to deliver the content. Ideas are not included for Standard 16. This standard deals with the diversity and communication in science which are implicit in many of the other structures. Each structure is effective for different learning objectives. With each new structure, we provide a new access route to the curriculum. If we are to be effective in achieving academic success with a diverse range of educational objectives in an increasingly diverse classroom, a diverse array of instructional strategies is essential. Being well-versed with a range of structures allows us to deliver the content masterfully and to provide high interest, novel, and motivating learning activities for our students. Mastering a range of structures empowers us as educators and opens up a world of possibilities for all our students to reach their potential.

Resources

• •

The following resources are the best sources available for more Kagan structures.

Kagan, Spencer. *Cooperative Learning.* San Clemente, CA: Kagan Publishing, 1994.

Kagan, S. & Kagan, M. *Multiple Intelligences: The Complete MI Book.* San Clemente, CA: Kagan Publishing, 1998.

Kagan, L., Kagan, M. & Kagan, S. *Teambuilding.* San Clemente, CA: Kagan Publishing, 1995.

Kagan, M. & Kagan, S. *Advanced Cooperative Learning: Playing with Elements.* San Clemente, CA: Kagan Publishing, 1993.

Kagan, M., Kagan, L. & Kagan, S. *Classbuilding.* San Clemente, CA: Kagan Publishing, 1995.

Table of Structures

Find My Rule

Students sharpen their inductive reasoning skills as they attempt to find the teacher's rule for placing items in different locations in a category system.

1 Teacher Places Item

The teacher decides on a category system. For example, the category system may be two boxes, one for things that are "hot" and the other for items that are "not hot." The teacher places the first item in one of the two boxes, but does not label the boxes or tell students the rule.

2 Think Time

The teacher calls for Think Time. Students attempt to uncover the "rule" for why the things are placed in separate boxes.

3 Students RallyRobin Rules

Students pair up with their shoulder partners. They take turns listing possible rules the teacher is using to place items in each box.

4 Teacher Places Next Items

The teacher places the next items in the boxes and provides think time again.

5 Students RallyRobin Rules

This time with their face partners, students take turns listing possible rules the teacher is using to place items in each box.

6 Teacher Places Next Items

The next items are placed in the boxes and students are given think time.

7 Team Discussion

Now, students as a team discuss the items placed and try to uncover the teacher's rule.

8 Students Generate Hypotheses

The teacher tells student teams to come up with items they think fit the category system.

9 Students Test Hypotheses

The teacher picks several teams to place the items they generated into the category system. Students are told not to state their rule, only to place their items. Each time items are placed, the teacher announces to the class if their hypothesis is correct or not. This continues with several teams until teams seem to know the rule.

VIDEO in the

We see Laurie Kagan using Find My Rule with 3rd graders to discover things that "Sink" and things that "Float." The ability to induce a rule, to make systematic observations which discredit competing hypotheses is fundamental to the scientific inquiry process. Find My Rule, regardless of the content, helps students reach the standards because they are engaging in inductive reasoning core to the scientific inquiry process.

10 Team Shares Rule

The teacher selects one team to share the rule with the class and confirms whether it is correct. If not, another team is selected to share.

11 Class Practice

The teacher announces the next item. Using choral practice or a show of fingers corresponding to the boxes, students respond to each new item for practice.

Find My Rule

Find My Rule
ADAPTATIONS

Inclusion

Physical Disabilities
Teachers should write or draw and verbally describe the items being placed in the category system.

Cognitive Disabilities
Students should be encouraged to give responses: "All ideas are helpful."

Behavioral or Emotional Disabilities
Overactive or uninhibited students tend to take over a class discussion and may need to have an individual agreement or contract with teacher for how many times they can respond. An individualized behavior contract that includes Talking Chips (students use a chip for every answer given; when they use all their chips they can't respond until the teacher replenishes the chips at a break) can be very effective to help "blurters" develop self-control.

ESL

Pre-Production to Speech Emergence
Use content that allows students to draw their responses.

Intermediate Fluency
No adaptations necessary.

reaching the
STANDARDS with *Find My Rule*

Standard 1

Earth & Space Sciences
Student knows the basic features of Earth.

Students induce the rule for:

• Characteristics of ocean water vs. fresh water.

• Things that happen in the summer vs. winter.

• Things that happen in the fall vs. spring.

• Characteristics or examples of solids vs. liquids.

• Examples of liquids vs. nonliquids.

• Things that are hot vs. cold.

Standard 2

Earth & Space Sciences
Student understands the basic processes of Earth.

Students induce the rule for:

• Changes caused by slow processes vs. quick processes.

• Changes that occur as a result of eroding vs. depositing.

• Characteristics or effects of a volcano vs. earthquake.

• Changes or effects of landslide vs. earthquake.

• Changes that occur as a result of wind vs. water.

Standard 3

Earth & Space Sciences
Student comprehends Earth's place in the universe and the essential composition and structure of the universe.

Students induce the rule for:

• Characteristics of the earth vs. the moon.

• Characteristics of star vs. planet.

• Characteristic of moon vs. sun.

• Characteristics of the Earth vs. Mars (or any two planets).

• Characteristics of satellite vs. moon.

• Things that are larger than the earth vs. things that are smaller than the earth.

reaching the
STANDARDS with *Find My Rule*

Standard 4

Life Sciences
Student understands the unity and diversity of life.

Students induce the rule for:

• Organisms that are mammals vs. organisms that are not mammals.

• Examples of living things that are plants vs. animals.

• Examples of things that are edible vs. things that are not edible.

• Examples of animals that are pets vs. animals that are not good pets.

• Examples of things that are living vs. nonliving.

• Example of animals that fly vs. don't fly.

Standard 5

Life Sciences
Student comprehends the basics of genetics.

Students induce the rule for:

• Things that are passed down from parent to offspring vs. things that are learned (nature vs. nurture).

Standard 6

Life Sciences
Student knows the structure and function of cells and organisms.

Students induce the rule for:

• Animals that breathe air with lungs vs. gills.

• Animals that are vertebrates vs. invertebrates.

• Processes that happen in the circulatory system vs. digestive system.

• Characteristics of an animal cell vs. plant cell.

• Things people do with hands vs. things people do with feet.

• Functions of one organ vs. those of another.

reaching the
STANDARDS with *Find My Rule*

Standard 7	Standard 8	Standard 9
Life Sciences	**Life Sciences**	**Life Sciences**
Student understands the interdependence of species and the environment.	*Student understands the role of matter and energy in the environment.*	*Student comprehends the basics of the evolution of species.*
Students induce the rule for:	*Students induce the rule for:*	*Students induce the rule for:*
• Examples or characteristics of predator vs. prey.	• Examples or characteristics of producers vs. consumers.	• Examples of animals that have become extinct vs. animals that are still living.
• Examples or characteristics of parasite vs. host.		• Examples of extinct vs. nonextinct plants.
• Examples of behavior motivated by internal cues (hunger) vs. external cues (changes in environment).		• Examples of animals that are endangered vs. animals that are thriving.

reaching the
STANDARDS with *Find My Rule*

Standard 10

Physical Sciences
Student understands the basic properties of matter.

Students induce the rule for:

- Things that are attracted by a magnet vs. not.

- Things that conduct electricity vs. things that don't.

- Things that are visible to the naked eye vs. things that aren't.

- Examples of elements vs. compounds.

- Things are soluble vs. things that are not soluble.

Standard 11

Physical Sciences
Student comprehends the types, sources, and conversions of energy and their relationship to heat and temperature.

Students induce the rule for:

- Things that produce light vs. things that don't.

- Things that are hot vs. things that are cold.

- Things that run on gas vs. things that use electricity.

- Things that produce heat vs. things that don't.

- Things that conduct heat well vs. things that don't.

Standard 12

Physical Sciences
Student comprehends the principles of motion.

Students induce the rule for:

- Things that move fast vs. things that move slowly.

- Things that move in a straight line vs. things that don't.

- Things that move in a circular motion vs. things that don't.

- Things that move as a result of compression vs. thrust.

- Things that are used to push vs. things that are used to pull.

- Things that move at a constant speed vs. things that move at a variable speed.

reaching the
STANDARDS with *Find My Rule*

Standard 13

Physical Sciences
Student understands the forces between objects and within atoms.

Students induce the rule for:

- Things a magnet will stick to vs. things it won't.

- Things that are held down by gravity vs. things that escape the earth's gravity.

Standard 14

Nature of Science
Student comprehends the nature of scientific knowledge.

Students induce the rule for:

- Things that can be replicated vs. things that can't.

Standard 15

Nature of Science
Student comprehends the nature of scientific inquiry.

Students induce the rule for:

- Things that can be answered with an experiment (cause) vs. things that can be answered by observation (description).

- Tools that are used by scientists vs. tools that are used by other professions.

Things That Float vs. Sink

Teacher Instructions: On the board, draw a "t" like the one below. Don't label the two columns. Add items and have students discuss them in pairs, then in teams, to find your rule: Things That Float vs. Things That Sink.

Things That Float	Things That Sink
Tree Branch	Rock
Boat	Car
Block of Wood	Metal
Cork	Computer
Balloon	Airplane
Surfboard	Brick
Raft	Anchor
Buoy	Weight Set
Life Jacket	Titanic

Mammals vs. Reptiles

Teacher Instructions: On the board, draw a "t" like the one below. Don't label the two columns. Add animals and have students discuss them in pairs, then in teams, to find your rule: Mammals vs. Reptiles.

Mammals	Reptiles
Cat	Iguana
Cow	Gecko
Monkey	Crocodile
Horse	Python
Giraffe	Gila Monster
Mouse	Chameleon
Lion	Alligator
Dog	Boa
Squirrel	Turtle

Similarity Groups

Students form groups to discover and discuss what they have in common with classmates.

1 Teacher Announces Topic

The teacher provides a topic on which students may group. The topic should be open-ended with a multitude of possible responses. For example, "If you could be any inventor, which inventor would you be?"

2 Students Think & Write

Students think of their response and write it down.

3 Students Form Similarity Groups

Students search for others that have the same or a similar response. They form a similarity group by huddling close together.

4 Teacher Announces Discussion Topic

The teacher announces a discussion topic. The topic is also open-ended with no right or wrong answer. For example, "Why did you choose the inventor you did?" or "What impact does her/his inventions have on us today?"

5 Partners Share

Students pair up to discuss the question. The structure Timed-Pair-Share works well to give each student an equal amount of time to share.

in the VIDEO

We watch Sally Scott demonstrate Similarity Groups with 1st graders. As students group common objects, they engage in one of the most basic tools of science. Before a dynamic understanding emerges, scientists strive for a taxonomic understanding. That is, they name and categorize objects and phenomena, whether they are the elements of the periodic table, types of clouds, or types of neuroses. In working with Similarity Groups, students are practicing science. They are doing what scientists do: categorizing and grouping objects and phenomena.

Similarity Groups

Similarity Groups
ADAPTATIONS

Inclusion

Physical Disabilities
Some students may need assistance in circulating or others need to come to them.

Cognitive Disabilities
A special education teacher or aide might assist students in creating their answers prior to the class session.

Behavioral or Emotional Disabilities
Prior to Similarity Groups, some students may need a reminder about " hands to self " or about maintaining respect for personal space.

ESL

Pre-Production & Early Production
Students each have a picture or drawing to categorize.

Speech Emergence & Intermediate Fluency
No adaptations necessary.

reaching the
STANDARDS with *Similarity Groups*

Standard 1

Earth & Space Sciences
Student knows the basic features of Earth.

Students form groups based on:

- Favorite summertime activity.

- Favorite thing to do in the snow.

- Favorite type of weather condition.

- Given cards with pictures or names with materials found on Earth, students form groups.

Standard 2

Earth & Space Sciences
Student understands the basic processes of Earth.

Students form groups based on:

- Response to which natural process (erosion, earthquake, landslides, volcanoes) have had the greatest impact on the earth's surface.

- Ideas on how to prevent erosion.

- Characteristics (size, shape, color, composition) of rocks or minerals provided.

Standard 3

Earth & Space Sciences
Student comprehends Earth's place in the universe and the essential composition and structure of the universe.

Students form groups based on:

- Planet they would most like to visit or study.

- Given cards with facts about planets and/or other celestial bodies, students form groups (based on distance from the sun, color, size, shape, temperature).

- Most interesting fact or phenomenon relating to Earth or the universe.

reaching the
STANDARDS with *Similarity Groups*

Standard 4

Life Sciences
Student understands the unity and diversity of life.

Students form groups based on:

- Favorite plant.

- Favorite animal.

- Given cards with pictures or names of animals on them, students form groups (based on pets, farm animals, mammals, birds, fishes, ocean animals).

- Given cards with pictures or names of plants on them, students form groups (based on flower, tree, color, size, evergreen, deciduous, habitat).

Standard 5

Life Sciences
Student comprehends the basics of genetics.

Students form groups based on:

- Strongest trait inherited from mother.

- Strongest trait inherited from father.

- Characteristics that are passed on from parent to offspring.

Standard 6

Life Sciences
Student knows the structure and function of cells and organisms.

Students form groups based on:

- Most important organ in the human body.

- Given cards with pictures or names of cells or organs, students form groups (based on system, function, location, size).

reaching the
STANDARDS with *Similarity Groups*

Standard 7

Life Sciences
Student understands the interdependence of species and the environment.

Students form groups based on:

- Greatest impact humans have had on the environment.

- Most important feature of the environment to support life.

- Place in the world it would be easiest (or most difficult) to survive.

- Animal humans depend on most.

- Animal that depends on humans most.

Standard 8

Life Sciences
Student understands the role of matter and energy in the environment.

Students form groups based on:

- Most fearsome predator.

- Animal with the most natural enemies.

- Most important source of energy for sustaining life on Earth other than the sun.

Standard 9

Life Sciences
Student comprehends the basics of the evolution of species.

Students form groups based on:

- Extinct animal they would most like to revive.

- Reason why dinosaurs became extinct.

reaching the
STANDARDS with *Similarity Groups*

Standard 10

Physical Sciences
Student understands the basic properties of matter.

Students form groups based on:

- Given actual materials such as cloth, paper, wood, metal or cards with pictures or names of such materials on them, students form groups (based on color, size, shape, weight).

- Given a variety of tools, students form groups (based on the type of simple machine, function, size, or shape).

Standard 11

Physical Sciences
Student comprehends the types, sources, and conversions of energy and their relationship to heat and temperature.

Students form groups based on:

- Things that give off heat.

- Things that produce light.

- Given a variety of wire samples, students form groups (based on gauge, insulation, conductivity, material, function).

- Given a variety of powered household objects (flashlight, lawn mower, radio) or cards with the names of such objects, students form groups based on the type of energy they require.

Standard 12

Physical Sciences
Student comprehends the principles of motion.

Students form groups based on:

- Given a variety of musical instruments, students form groups (based on the sounds they produce, how they produce sounds, or their category: string, percussion, woodwind, brass).

- Given cards with the names or pictures of a variety of things that move (yo-yo, car, drill) students form groups based on how they move, the speed they move at, the direction they move.

reaching the
STANDARDS with *Similarity Groups*

Standard 13

Physical Sciences
Student understands the forces between objects and within atoms.

Students form groups based on:

- The force they think is most fascinating.

- The most useful force to humans.

Standard 14

Nature of Science
Student comprehends the nature of scientific knowledge.

Students form groups based on:

- What they thought was the hardest part of the experiment.

- The results of the same experiment performed by different teams or individuals (should normally produce the same result, but results may vary).

- Given cards with the names of scientists studied, students form groups based on similarities (when they lived, their field, the importance of their contribution).

Standard 15

Nature of Science
Student comprehends the nature of scientific inquiry.

Students form groups based on:

- Given a variety of scientific instruments (thermometers, magnifiers, rulers, balances) students form groups based on their uses.

- Given a variety of scientific discoveries or inventions, students form groups based on how they came about, why needed, when they occurred.

Observe-Draw-RallyRobin

Students record their observations of an item by drawing the item. Students then take turns sharing with a partner their observations from their drawings.

1 Teacher Provides Item

The teacher provides an item for students to draw. For example, the item may be a model of the solar system. The teacher may provide hints about how to observe and what to draw.

2 Students Draw

While observing, each student creates a visual record of his or her observations by silently drawing the object. The drawings don't have to be realistic. They can be symbolic or personally meaningful.

3 Object Hidden

The object or item is placed out of students' view.

in the
VIDEO

4 Partners RallyRobin

With the object or item out of view, students pair up and use their own drawings to make comments about their observations. Partner A makes the first comment, "The sun is the biggest thing." Partner B makes the next observation, "The planets are all around the Sun." Students continue taking turns describing observations for a predetermined amount of time.

5 Team Discussion

The object is returned so students can all see it again. As a team, students discuss their drawings, what they missed, and what new observations they have.

We watch Lee Lin-Brande demonstrate the structure Observe-Draw-RallyRobin with 3rd graders using peanuts as the content. Perhaps the most important of all science process skills is observation. Careful observation leads to the generation and evaluation of alternative hypotheses. Many great scientific discoveries spring from systematic observation. In fact, the scientific inquiry process itself is based on systematic, controlled observation. Thus as students use the Observe-Draw-RallyRobin structure, they are developing the science process skills.

Observe-Draw-RallyRobin

Observe-Draw-RallyRobin
ADAPTATIONS

Inclusion

Physical Disabilities
Students with fine motor coordination difficulties will not be able to complete this task. They might think of words that describe the object to share with the group. They might hold or touch the object, depending on their disability, so they have a better concept of what the other students are observing and drawing.

Cognitive Disabilities
This structure may be a strength for some students because it does not depend as much on written and oral language. Students may be pretaught descriptive words and phrases to use for discussion.

Behavioral or Emotional Disabilities
Students may benefit from preteaching of impulse control and focusing techniques.

ESL

Pre-Production & Early Production
Students at these levels need partners who are at Speech Emergence or Intermediate Fluency. Do the RallyRobin step between pairs on the team rather than within pairs.

Speech Emergence & Intermediate Fluency
No adaptations necessary.

reaching the
STANDARDS with *Observe-Draw-RallyRobin*

Standard 1

Earth & Space Sciences
Student knows the basic features of Earth.

Students observe, draw, and RallyRobin discuss:

- A drop of water under the microscope.

- The weather outside on different days.

- Ice melting.

- Water evaporating.

- Water condensing in a covered container.

- Soil samples.

- Rocks or minerals.

- Liquids.

Standard 2

Earth & Space Sciences
Student understands the basic processes of Earth.

Students observe, draw, and RallyRobin discuss:

- A picture of an eroded mountain or landscape.

- Fossil of a plant or animal.

- Post-earthquake scene.

- Picture of the effects of a tornado or hurricane.

- Video of the eruption of a volcano, the flow of lava, and the cooling of the lava.

- Tidal wave.

Standard 3

Earth & Space Sciences
Student comprehends Earth's place in the universe and the essential composition and structure of the universe.

Students observe, draw, and RallyRobin discuss:

- The earth from space.

- A picture of the solar system.

- Planet.

- Constellation.

- The shadow of an object at various times during the day.

- Celestial bodies.

- Objects with a telescope or tube planetarium.

reaching the
STANDARDS with *Observe-Draw-RallyRobin*

Standard 4

Life Sciences
Student understands the unity and diversity of life.

Students observe, draw, and RallyRobin discuss:

- Plant.

- Animal.

- Plant or animal at different stages of life (caterpillar and butterfly).

- Flower.

- Insect with magnifying glass.

- Pictures of two similar animals and insects (dolphin and whale, butterfly and moth).

Standard 5

Life Sciences
Student comprehends the basics of genetics.

Students observe, draw, and RallyRobin discuss:

- Parent and offspring of a pet.

- Picture of a classmate with mother or father.

- Tree and sapling.

- Thumbprint.

Standard 6

Life Sciences
Student knows the structure and function of cells and organisms.

Students observe, draw, and RallyRobin discuss:

- Plant or animal cell under a microscope.

- Leaf.

- Entire plant with roots intact.

- Picture illustrating the arrangement of internal organs, muscles, or arteries and veins.

- Skeleton model.

- Teammate's hand, foot, ear, or nose.

reaching the
STANDARDS with *Observe-Draw-RallyRobin*

Standard 7

Life Sciences
Student understands the interdependence of species and the environment.

Students observe, draw, and RallyRobin discuss:

- Interdependent animals.

- Parasite on a host.

- Animal eating or drinking.

- Plant without adequate water or sunlight.

- Undernourished animal or person.

Standard 8

Life Sciences
Student understands the role of matter and energy in the environment.

Students observe, draw, and RallyRobin discuss:

- Picture of plant or animal depending on any natural resource (food, water, light, or air).

- Diagram of a food chain or food web.

Standard 9

Life Sciences
Student comprehends the basics of the evolution of species.

Students observe, draw, and RallyRobin discuss:

- A picture illustrating the evolution of species.

- Fossil.

reaching the
STANDARDS with *Observe-Draw-RallyRobin*

Standard 10

Physical Sciences
Student understands the basic properties of matter.

Students observe, draw, and RallyRobin discuss:

- Different materials as seen by eye, magnifying glass, or microscope:
  - Cloth
  - Paper
  - Wood
  - Metal
  - Rusted metal
  - Rock
  - Glass
  - Powder
  - Salt

Students pay special attention to size, shape, color, and structure.

Standard 11

Physical Sciences
Student comprehends the types, sources, and conversions of energy and their relationship to heat and temperature.

Students observe, draw, and RallyRobin discuss:

- Fire burning.

- Different materials exposed to fire.

- Organization of an electrical circuit.

Standard 12

Physical Sciences
Student comprehends the principles of motion.

Students observe, draw, and RallyRobin discuss:

- Object's motion in relation to its position over time.

- Objects in motion:
  - Ball
  - Yo-yo
  - Person walking
  - Insect crawling
  - Bicycle
  - Flight pattern of a paper airplane
  - Tree in the wind

reaching the
STANDARDS *with Observe-Draw-RallyRobin*

Standard 13

Physical Sciences
Student understands the forces between objects and within atoms.

Students observe, draw, and RallyRobin discuss:

- The same object twice and compare results of the first observation with those of the second observation. Are they the same? Was anything new or different discovered?

- Students compare observations of the same object by different observers to learn that observations collected by different people may give different results.

Standard 14

Nature of Science
Student comprehends the nature of scientific knowledge.

Students observe, draw, and RallyRobin discuss:

- Scientific tools:
  - Thermometers
  - Balances
  - Burners
  - Beakers
  - Scales
  - Rulers

Standard 15

Nature of Science
Student comprehends the nature of scientific inquiry.

All observations can be linked to this standard as the nature of careful observation is part of the scientific inquiry process.

Songs for Two Voices

In pairs, students sing a song. Partners sing some lines alone and some lines in unison.

1 Teacher Prepares Song

The teacher prepares the lyrics to a curriculum song for students. For example, the song may include facts about dinosaurs. Some lines are marked with "A," and others with "B," and others yet with "AB."

2 Teacher Explains Directions

The teacher has students pair up. One partner is an A and the other a B. The teacher explains that A's sing when the line is marked with "A." B's sing when the line is marked with "B." They sing in unison for lines marked "AB."

3 Students Sing Songs

Students sing their part, keeping pace with their partners.

Vin theIDEO

Karen Karst-Hoskins demonstrates the structure Songs for Two Voices with 2nd graders. Students sing a song about the water cycle to review what they've learned. A Song for Two Voices engages the musical/rhythmic intelligence. The content, the water cycle, helps reach the standard of understanding basic earth processes.

Variations

Songs for More Voices
Songs may be sung in pairs, in teams (2 A's and 2 B's), or as a whole class (half A's and half B's).

Student Roles
Students may be given the lyrics to a song and may come up with their own division of roles.

Student Songs
Students may make up their own songs.

Student Choreography
Students may incorporate movement or gestures to add a bodily/kinesthetic dimension to the song.

Songs for Two Voices

Songs for Two Voices

ADAPTATIONS

Inclusion

Physical Disabilities
Students who are physically unable to sing the words might use a simple instrument (such as a rattle, tambourine, or striking sticks) for their part.

Cognitive Disabilities
Students may need to practice or read the lines with a peer or the teacher prior to the activity.

Behavioral or Emotional Disabilities
Students should be able to fully participate.

ESL

Pre-Production & Early Production
Pre-Productive students can be buddies that observe their partners and point to words as they sing them.

Speech Emergence & Intermediate Fluency
No adaptations necessary.

reaching the
STANDARDS with *Songs for Two Voices*

Standard 1

Earth & Space Sciences
Student knows the basic features of Earth.

Students write and/or sing songs about:

• Tiny Droplets: A song about clouds and fog made of tiny drops of water.

• Round and Round: A song about the water cycle.

• Oceans and Lakes: A song about the characteristics of oceans and lakes.

• You Are My Sunshine: A song about the light and heat the sun provides.

• Spinning in Space: A song about Earth's rotation on its axis causes day and night and its orbit around the sun causes winter and summer.

Standard 2

Earth & Space Sciences
Student understands the basic processes of Earth.

Students write and/or sing songs about:

• Shake, Rattle & Roll: A song about earthquakes and their effects on Earth's surface.

• Changes: A song about the constant changes to the earth's surface caused by processes such as weathering, erosion, waves, wind, water, ice, volcanic eruptions, and earthquakes.

• The Rock Song: A song about the processes of the rock cycle — erosion, transport, and deposit.

Standard 3

Earth & Space Sciences
Student comprehends Earth's place in the universe and the essential composition and structure of the universe.

Students write and/or sing songs about:

• High in the Sky: A song about the use of telescopes to see and magnify distant objects in the sky.

• Phases of the Moon: A song explaining why the moon appears to change shape throughout the month.

• Solar System: A song about the location, size, and composition of planets in the solar system.

reaching the
STANDARDS with *Songs for Two Voices*

Standard 4

Life Sciences

Student understands the unity and diversity of life.

Students write and/or sing songs about:

- Unity of Life: A song about the commonalities animals share.

- Diversity of Life: A song about the differences among animals.

- From the Cradle to the Grave: A song about the life cycle of humans.

- Categories of Life: A song about the categories in which living organisms can be grouped (plants, animals, mammals, reptiles, fish, or birds).

Standard 5

Life Sciences

Student comprehends the basics of genetics.

Students write and/or sing songs about:

- I'm Like Mom or Pop: A song about the inherited characteristics students receive from their parent(s).

- How I'm Unique: A song about the differences among individuals and how students are each unique.

- What's Genetic & What's Not: A song about what characteristics that are inherited (eye color) vs. characteristics that are learned (ability to play soccer).

Standard 6

Life Sciences

Student knows the structure and function of cells and organisms.

Students write and/or sing songs about:

- Systems of the Body: A song about the systems of the body and their basic functions (or about a single system).

- What We Need to Survive: A song about the basic needs of animals (air, water, food, shelter); or the needs of plants (air, water, nutrients, light).

- The Heart Song: A song about the structure and function of the heart (or any other organ being studied).

reaching the
STANDARDS with *Songs for Two Voices*

Standard 7

Life Sciences
Student understands the interdependence of species and the environment.

Students write and/or sing songs about:

- The Food Chain: A song about how plants and animals depend on each other.

- Foods I Love: A song about foods students love and the plants and animals from which they come.

- Life in the Forest: A song about the effects a habitat has on plant or animal life.

- My Little Friends: The positive relationship of microorganisms and humans.

Standard 8

Life Sciences
Student understands the role of matter and energy in the environment.

Students write and/or sing songs about:

- The Energy Around Me: A song about the transfer of energy from the sun to plants to animals to humans.

- What I Really Need: A song about what students really need to survive and where they get the resources (breathe air, eat food, drink water). Can include what I really want vs. need.

Standard 9

Life Sciences
Student comprehends the basics of the evolution of species.

Students write and/or sing songs about:

- The T-Rex Rap: A rap about the mighty carnivore, when it lived, how big it was, what it did to survive, what it ate, and why it is not alive today. (May also be about any specific dinosaur or dinosaurs in general.)

- Endangered Species: A song about an endangered species (panda, whooping crane, orangutan, spectacled bear, bald eagle, or giant armadillo).

- Evolution: A song about the "survival of the fittest."

reaching the
STANDARDS with *Songs for Two Voices*

Standard 10

Physical Sciences
Student understands the basic properties of matter.

Students write and/or sing songs about:

- Materials That Matter: A song about the characteristics of common materials such as wood, metal, plastic, cloth, or rubber.

- Changing States Chant: A chant about the different states of matter (solid, liquid, and gas) and how to change matter from state to state.

- Too Small for the Eye: A song about the particles of matter that are too small to be seen by the naked eye.

Standard 11

Physical Sciences
Student comprehends the types, sources, and conversions of energy and their relationship to heat and temperature.

Students write and/or sing songs about:

- Simple Circuit Song: A song about the basic organization of a simple circuit.

- Funky Heat Beat: A song about things that are hot and their sources of heat.

- Energy Around Me: A song about the transformation and conservation of energy.

- Packed with Power: A song about the various sources of energy (battery, generator, electrical, or mechanical).

Standard 12

Physical Sciences
Student comprehends the principles of motion.

Students write and/or sing songs about:

- The Sounds All Around: A song about the sounds we often hear and how they are produced by vibrations and their pitch depends on the frequency of the vibration.

- Light in Sight: A song about the characteristics of the motion of light including its speed, its direction, and how light can be refracted, reflected, or absorbed.

- Moving & Grooving: A song about things in motion, their direction of movement, and the forces needed to speed up, slow down, or change directions.

reaching the
STANDARDS with *Songs for Two Voices*

Standard 13

Physical Sciences
Student understands the forces between objects and within atoms.

Students write and/or sing songs about:

• Gravity and Me: A song about the characteristics of gravity and how it influences our lives.

• I'm Stuck on You: A song about the characteristics of magnets (why they attract and repel each other, what they stick to, and what they won't).

Standard 14

Nature of Science
Student comprehends the nature of scientific knowledge.

Students write and/or sing songs about:

• The Nature of Knowledge: A song about the scientific process and how information is gained through investigations that produce similar results when carried out in other times, places, and by other people.

Standard 15

Nature of Science
Student comprehends the nature of scientific inquiry.

Students write and/or sing songs about:

• How We Know What We Know: A song about how scientific learning comes from observations and experiments done by scientists.

• The Tools of the Trade: A song about the tools scientists use and what they are used for.

The Water Cycle Songs

Instructions: With a partner, sing the songs below. Partner A sings the A lines. Partner B sings the B lines. Sing the AB lines in unison.

Drip from the Sky

To the tune of "Row, Row, Row Your Boat"

AB	Drip, drip, drip from the sky into a little stream
AB	Down the mountains
AB	Through the plains
AB	And out into the sea.
A	Up, up, up it goes
B	Up into the sky
A	Over the mountains
B	It blows again,
AB	Snowflakes watch them fly.

Around and Around

To the tune of "My Darling Clementine"

A	Evaporation
B	Condensation
AB	Precipitation falling down
A	These are all parts of
B	The water cycle
AB	It just goes
AB	Around and around.

F.O.R.C.E

Instructions: With a partner, sing the song below. Partner A sings the A lines.
Partner B sings the B lines. Sing the AB lines in unison.

To the tune of "Bingo"

A	A force can be a gentle nudge
B	Like pushing 'gainst a rocker
A	F.O.R.C.E.
B	F.O.R.C.E.
AB	F.O.R.C.E.
AB	A force can be a small nudge!

B	A strong push helps when things won't budge
A	Like moving trains and tractors
B	F.O.R.C.E.
A	F.O.R.C.E.
AB	F.O.R.C.E.
AB	A force can be a strong shove!

A	A force can be a gentle tug
B	Like pulling up a yo-yo
A	F.O.R.C.E.
B	F.O.R.C.E.
AB	F.O.R.C.E.
AB	A force can be a small tug!

B	A great big crane is used to lug
A	Huge beams and bricks or lumber
B	F.O.R.C.E.
A	F.O.R.C.E.
AB	F.O.R.C.E.
AB	A force can be a strong tug!

A	When you pedal up a hill
B	You push the pedals harder
A	P.U.S.H. HARD!
B	P.U.S.H. HARD!
AB	P.U.S.H. HARD!
AB	A strong force takes you farther!

B	A push or pull can change the speed
A	Of something that needs movin'
B	F.O.R.C.E.
A	F.O.R.C.E.
AB	F.O.R.C.E.
AB	These forces are worth usin'!

A	One horse can't pull a heavy load
B	But give the horse some credit
A	M.O.R.E. HORSE
B	M.O.R.E. HORSE
AB	M.O.R.E. HORSE
AB	More horse, more force!…you get it?

B	A force can change the size or shape
A	Of things like silly putty
B	F.O.R.C.E.
A	F.O.R.C.E.
AB	F.O.R.C.E.
AB	Don't use force on somebody!!!

From Lyrical Lessons by Clint Klose & Larry Wolfe
© 1997 Kagan Publishing

Same-Different

Teams are given two similar items, one for each pair. Without seeing the other pair's item, they try to uncover everything that is the same and different about the two items. Same-Different builds analytic skills.

1 Teams Uncover Similarities and Differences

In a team of four, two students sit on one side of a barrier and the other two on the other side. Each pair has a slightly different picture or item. For example, one pair may have a moth specimen or picture and the other pair may have a butterfly specimen or picture. Without divulging what their item is, pairs discuss their items to uncover similarities and differences.

2 Pairs Record Similarities and Differences

Each pair has a recording sheet with space to record the things that are the "Same" and things that are "Different." Partners take turns recording each new discovery.

VIDEO in the

Science

We see Denise Gordon using Same-Different with 1st graders finding the similarities and differences between two pictures on outer space. Scientists spend a great deal of effort comparing and contrasting objects and phenomena — whether it is alligators and crocodiles, physical elements, or reactions of different people to stimuli. As students compare and contrast Same-Different pictures, they hone their observation and analytic thinking skills.

Variations

Pair Same-Different

Students can work in pairs rather than as a team. In pairs, each partner gets a different picture or object to describe. Both students record each similarity and difference.

Alternative Interactions

Many forms of student interaction are possible for students to discover what's the same and what's different:

- talking
- writing notes
- writing essays about the pictures
- drawing pictures to pass to each other
- acting out the pictures
- discussing the pictures from memory with pictures out of sight

Same-Different

Same-Different
ADAPTATIONS

Inclusion

Physical Disabilities
A peer may assist in asking questions and/or recording answers as a student with disabilities points to parts of the picture or object.

Cognitive Disabilities
The difficulty of the task should be within the cognitive capacity of all students. Students with learning disabilities may find and record fewer similarities and differences.

Behavioral or Emotional Disabilities
When the pictures or items being compared contain many easily identifiable similarities and differences, frustration levels remain low.

ESL

Pre-Production & Early Production
Pre-Productive students can be buddies that observe their partners point to pictures of words used.

Speech Emergence & Intermediate Fluency
No adaptations necessary.

reaching the
STANDARDS with *Same-Different*

Standard 1

Earth & Space Sciences
Student knows the basic features of Earth.

Students discover the similarities and differences between:

- Fresh water and salt water, using descriptions of the characteristics of each.

- Fall and winter using pictures of each season (or any two seasons).

- Rainy day and a sunny day using a sample of each picture or illustration (or any two weather patterns).

- Day and night using any two pictures of the earth on its axis in relation to the sun.

Standard 2

Earth & Space Sciences
Student understands the basic processes of Earth.

Students discover the similarities and differences between:

- Different rocks or minerals using two different samples of each.

- Different types of soil or sand samples using two different samples of each.

- The effects of an earthquake and the effects of a volcanic eruption using pictures of the aftermath of each.

- An animal and plant fossil using samples of each.

- Any two fossils.

Standard 3

Earth & Space Sciences
Student comprehends Earth's place in the universe and the essential composition and structure of the universe.

Students discover the similarities and differences between:

- The sun and the moon using pictures or descriptions of each.

- Saturn and Jupiter or any two planets.

- Two different constellations or star patterns in different seasons.

- Modern telescope and old telescope using a diagram of each.

- Current and ancient understanding of the universe using written descriptions.

reaching the
STANDARDS with *Same-Different*

Standard 4

Life Sciences
Student understands the unity and diversity of life.

Students discover the similarities and differences between:

- A human and a chimpanzee using a photograph of each.

- A shark and a dolphin using a description or picture of each.

- Any two different plants or flowers.

- The skeletal structure of any two mammals.

- A spider and an insect.

- A frog and a toad.

- An alligator and a crocodile.

Standard 5

Life Sciences
Student comprehends the basics of genetics.

Students discover the similarities and differences between:

- Two different thumbprints, handprints, or footprints.

- Two animals of different species.

- Two plants of the same species.

- An adult and the offspring of an animal or plant.

- Student and his/her parent using a photograph of each.

Standard 6

Life Sciences
Student knows the structure and function of cells and organisms.

Students discover the similarities and differences between:

- The cellular structure of a plant and animal using a diagram of each.

- Any two cells.

- A description of a single-celled organism and a multicellular organism.

- Two different leaves or leaf rubbings.

- A hand and a foot.

- A wing on a bird and a fin on a fish.

reaching the
STANDARDS with *Same-Different*

Standard 7

Life Sciences

Student understands the interdependence of species and the environment.

Students discover the similarities and differences between:

- Two different habitats using pictures or descriptions, including:
  - Climate
  - Location
  - Animals
  - Plants

- Any two animals and their dependence on their natural environment.

Standard 8

Life Sciences

Student understands the role of matter and energy in the environment.

Students discover the similarities and differences between:

- Two different pictures of plants or animals that depend on natural resources for energy.

- Any two different food chain or food web diagrams.

Standard 9

Life Sciences

Student comprehends the basics of the evolution of species.

Students discover the similarities and differences between:

- Description of any two endangered species.

- A present-day animal and its ancient relative.

- Two similar animals that evolved in different geographical locations (African elephant and Indian elephant).

reaching the
STANDARDS with *Same-Different*

Standard 10

Physical Sciences
Student understands the basic properties of matter.

Students discover the similarities and differences between:

- A piece of wood and piece of plastic (or any two different types of materials).

- Two different mixtures.

- An object before and after it is exposed to heat (piece of bread and toast).

- Two different scientific tools.

- Two different liquids (water and juice).

- Any classroom items. Students describe them in terms of their physical characteristics and composition.

Standard 11

Physical Sciences
Student comprehends the types, sources, and conversions of energy and their relationship to heat and temperature.

Students discover the similarities and differences between:

- Two circuits arranged differently.

- A nine-volt and a twelve-volt battery or any two different batteries.

- A kerosene lamp and an electric lamp.

- A toothbrush and an electric toothbrush (or any other two similar items that rely on different sources of energy).

Standard 12

Physical Sciences
Student comprehends the principles of motion.

Students discover the similarities and differences between:

- Pictures of two different roller coaster rides.

- The same object in motion from two different perspectives relative to a background.

- An airplane and a helicopter.

- A bicycle and a motorcycle.

- A rowboat and a sailboat.

- A football and a soccer ball.

reaching the
STANDARDS with *Same-Different*

Standard 13

Physical Sciences
Student understands the forces between objects and within atoms.

Students discover the similarities and differences between:

- The magnetic fields of two different magnets using paper and iron filings.

- Two pictures, one showing a scene in which gravity is present and one showing a scene without gravity.

Standard 14

Nature of Science
Student comprehends the nature of scientific knowledge.

Students discover the similarities and differences between:

- A scientist and an engineer.

- An astronomer and oceanographer.

- A biologist and a chemist.

- A physicist and a botanist.

Standard 15

Nature of Science
Student comprehends the nature of scientific inquiry.

Students discover the similarities and differences between:

- A description of an observation and a description of an experiment.

- A magnifying glass and a telescope.

- A microscope and a telescope.

- A ruler and a thermometer.

Outer Space

Picture 1

Instructions: List 15 similarities and 15 differences with your partner's picture. Do not look at each other's picture until you are done and ready to compare.

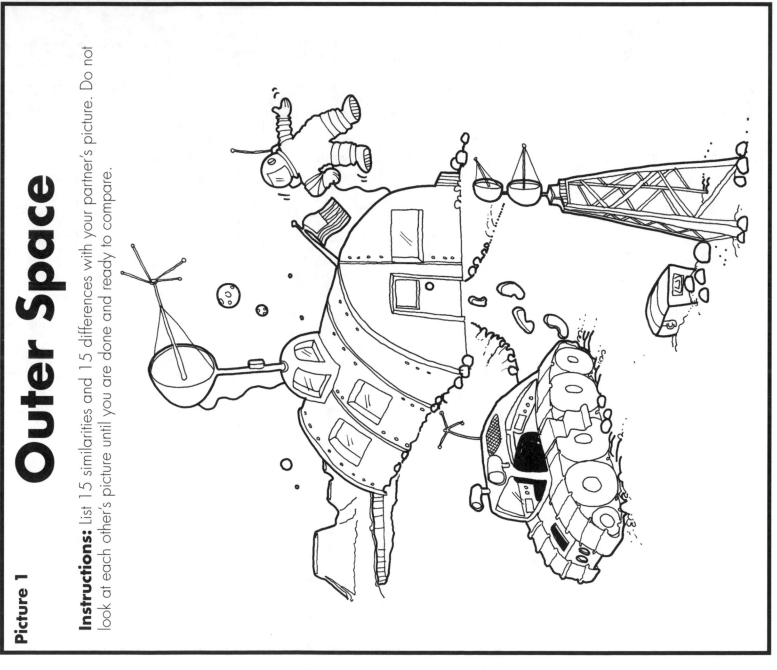

Picture 2

Outer Space

Instructions: List 15 similarities and 15 differences with your partner's picture. Do not look at each other's picture until you are done and ready to compare.

Space Station

Outer Space Recording Sheet

SAME	DIFFERENT
1. _____	1. _____
2. _____	2. _____
3. _____	3. _____
4. _____	4. _____
5. _____	5. _____
6. _____	6. _____
7. _____	7. _____
8. _____	8. _____
9. _____	9. _____
10. _____	10. _____
11. _____	11. _____
12. _____	12. _____
13. _____	13. _____
14. _____	14. _____
15. _____	15. _____

Outer Space Key

Key of differences.

1. **Location of planets**
2. **Number of planets**
3. **Location of footsteps**
4. **Number of chests**
5. **Color of space mobile's tires**
6. **Bolts on space station**
7. **Antenna on space mobile**
8. **Windows on space station**

9. **Number of astronauts**
10. **Craters under astronaut**
11. **Color of astronaut's suit**
12. **Color of space station**
13. **Flag on space station**
14. **Rocks behind space mobile**
15. **Sign on space station**

Team Mind Mapping

Students work in teams to symbolize the content with this visual/spatial, relational format. Comprehension, higher-level thinking, and retention are enhanced.

1 Teacher Provides Topic

The teacher announces the topic for teams to mind map. Mind Mapping works well for a wide variety of science topics, from large branches of science (astronomy, physics, life science, health), to specific topics of study (magnets, plants, electricity), to scientists (Edison, Pasteur, Galileo), to processes (water cycle, experimental process, lab procedures).

2 Teammates Brainstorm Main Ideas

The team writes or draws the central image in the center of the team's page (preferably large butcher paper). Then they brainstorm the main concepts relating to the central image and write them or draw images or symbols to represent the related ideas. Students use branches, arrows, or spokes to connect the main ideas to the central concept.

3 Teammates Add Details

Teammates use color, key words, bold letters, pictures, symbols, arrows, and connections to illustrate their team mind maps.

We view Kathryn Pugh using Team Mind Mapping with 5th graders to create mind maps on inventions relating to technology and communication. The content, inventions, acquaints students with the history of scientific applications which have led to technological advances. The structure, Mind Mapping, engages students with yet another way to organize information. As students organize the content with a Mind Map, they practice categorizing skills that are a core part of the scientific inquiry process.

Management Tips

Different Colors
Increase individual accountability by having each student use a different color marker or pen. This makes it easy for teammates and the teacher to see the contribution of each student.

Prime the Pump
As a class or in teams, have students discuss or brainstorm ideas so they each have things to add to the team mind map.

Pictures Only
Students can do mind maps using pictures only. When they are done, they discuss the symbols and pictures they used and what they represent.

Team Mind Mapping

Team Mind Mapping
ADAPTATIONS

Inclusion

Physical Disabilities
It is difficult for some physically challenged students to share physical space and produce work on a common team paper. Those students may need to work individually on a symbol, word, or picture to add to the paper.

Cognitive Disabilities
Some students may make oral contributions while teammates write or draw for the student. Some students have the most difficulty working with students with disabilities when it affects the product that the group is producing. Students need to learn contributions by all are valued.

Behavioral or Emotional Disabilities
The close proximity in this structure can be difficult for some students. If necessary, students can take a step back for a "breather" to reduce stress.

ESL

Pre-Production
Use content that will allow students to draw ideas.

Early Production
Review and post vocabulary related to the theme.

Speech Emergence & Intermediate Fluency
No adaptations necessary.

reaching the
STANDARDS with *Team Mind Mapping*

Standard 1

Earth & Space Sciences
Student knows the basic features of Earth.

Teams create a mind map of:

• States of water.

• Clouds.

• Seasons.

• Air.

• Daytime.

• The sun.

• The water cycle.

• Weather.

• Earth.

• Rocks.

Standard 2

Earth & Space Sciences
Student understands the basic processes of Earth.

Teams create a mind map of:

• Volcano.

• Earthquake.

• Hurricane.

• Changes on earth's surface.

• Erosion.

• Waves.

• Wind.

Standard 3

Earth & Space Sciences
Student comprehends Earth's place in the universe and the essential composition and structure of the universe.

Teams create a mind map of:

• Universe.

• Sun.

• Solar system.

• Jupiter.

• Moon.

• Outer space.

• Stars.

reaching the
STANDARDS with *Team Mind Mapping*

Standard 4

Life Sciences
Student understands the unity and diversity of life.

Teams create a mind map of:

• Pets.

• Animals.

• Insects.

• Life.

• Unity of life.

• Diversity of life.

• Life cycles.

• Animal classification.

• Plant classification.

Standard 5

Life Sciences
Student comprehends the basics of genetics.

Teams create a mind map of:

• Genetics.

• Principles of heredity.

• Mendel's Law.

• DNA.

• Reproduction.

Standard 6

Life Sciences
Student knows the structure and function of cells and organisms.

Teams create a mind map of:

• Survival.

• Cells.

• Growth.

• Reproduction.

• Systems.

• Organs.

reaching the
STANDARDS with *Team Mind Mapping*

Standard 7	Standard 8	Standard 9
Life Sciences *Student understands the interdependence of species and the environment.*	**Life Sciences** *Student understands the role of matter and energy in the environment.*	**Life Sciences** *Student comprehends the basics of the evolution of species.*
Teams create a mind map of:	Teams create a mind map of:	Teams create a mind map of:
• Why study plants?	• Food chain.	• Evolution.
• Environments.	• Food web.	• Extinction.
• Changes.	• Recycling.	• Dinosaurs.
• Interdependence.	• Energy.	• Endangered species.
	• Matter.	• Fossils.
	• Resources for survival.	• Survival.

reaching the
STANDARDS with *Team Mind Mapping*

Standard 10

Physical Sciences
Student understands the basic properties of matter.

Teams create a mind map of:

• States of matter.

• Magnets.

• Parts of a house.

• Solubility.

• Conductivity.

• Density.

• Properties of _____.
  (Fill in any type of material.)

Standard 11

Physical Sciences
Student comprehends the types, sources, and conversions of energy and their relationship to heat and temperature.

Teams create a mind map of:

• Heat.

• Electricity.

• Transformation.

• Conservation.

• What makes things work.

• Thermodynamics.

Standard 12

Physical Sciences
Student comprehends the principles of motion.

Teams create a mind map of:

• Force.

• Newton.

• Motion.

• Principles of motion.

• Simple machines.

reaching the
STANDARDS with *Team Mind Mapping*

Standard 13	Standard 14	Standard 15
Physical Sciences ***Student understands the forces between objects and within atoms.*** *Teams create a mind map of:* • Gravity. • Galileo. • Magnets. • Atoms. • Force.	**Nature of Science** ***Student comprehends the nature of scientific knowledge.*** *Teams create a mind map of:* • Inventions. • Inventors.	**Nature of Science** ***Student comprehends the nature of scientific inquiry.*** *Teams create a mind map of:* • Scientific tools. • The scientific method. • Experiments. • Observations.

RoundTable

In teams, students take turns generating written or drawn responses, or responses with manipulatives.

1 Teacher Assigns Topic

The teacher assigns a topic, question, problem or project with multiple answers, solutions, or that can be completed in multiple rounds. For example, a question may be: "What are some things you use that depend on electricity?" A project may be, "Draw a model of the human skeleton. Draw just one bone on the model as the paper comes to you."

2 Students Take Turns

In teams, each student makes a contribution to the team list or project.

Variation

Praise-N-Pass

Use this variation to promote social skills and a more positive tone in the team. Before passing the paper or project, or before the next teammate makes his/her contribution to the science project, he/she must offer a praiser to the teammate who just contributed. "Oh, that's good. It's really starting to look like the solar system now."

Management Tips

Different Colors

Increase individual accountability by having each student use a different color marker or pen. This makes it easy for teammates and the teacher to see the contribution of each student.

Taking Turns

RoundTable is a turn-taking structure that works very well for getting all students to actively participate. Use this structure with projects and experiments.

in the VIDEO

We see Karen Karst-Hoskins using RoundTable with 2nd graders. Students take turns writing an answer to open-ended questions about ecology: "How can kids help save the environment? What can each of us do?" These questions, addressed via RoundTable, place science in a personal and social perspective. Round-Table helps students understand our interdependence; each of us contributes to maintaining a healthy ecological balance.

RoundTable

RoundTable
ADAPTATIONS

Inclusion

Physical Disabilities
Some students may need a scribe (peer or aide) for writing answers.

Cognitive Disabilities
Some students may write a shortened answer, draw a picture, circle an answer, or make a smaller contribution to the team project. Some students may need a longer time to answer or to do their part. Peers need to practice the skill of patient waiting.

Behavioral or Emotional Disabilities
Encouraging and praising students or, practicing Praise-N-Pass are helpful in keeping some students focused and motivated.

ESL

Pre-Production
Use manipulatives and content that allows students to draw their responses.

Early Production
Use Cooperative Reading Boards, review vocabulary associated with particular themes, i.e. solar system, anatomy, etc.

Speech Emergence to Intermediate Fluency
No adaptations necessary.

reaching the
STANDARDS with RoundTable

Standard 1

Earth & Space Sciences
Student knows the basic features of Earth.

Teammates take turns:

- Listing things that are in a liquid state (or gas or solid state).

- Drawing the stages of the water cycle.

- Reading about the effect the sun has on the earth (or any reading relating to the features of the earth).

- Listing materials that are made of metal (plastic, rubber, wood, or cloth).

- Listing things that happen in the summer (winter, spring, or fall).

Standard 2

Earth & Space Sciences
Student understands the basic processes of Earth.

Teammates take turns:

- Listing processes that change the earth's surface.

- Drawing different landforms.

- Listing things that have changed on earth over time.

- Listing minerals studied.

- Sequencing things that would happen as a result of a tidal wave.

- Writing facts that they learned about volcanoes.

Standard 3

Earth & Space Sciences
Student comprehends Earth's place in the universe and the essential composition and structure of the universe.

Teammates take turns:

- Listing things that they wonder about the universe.

- Listing the characteristics of a particular planet.

- Sequencing the planets in the solar system by distance from sun (or size).

- Recording interesting observations about the moon.

- Figuring the relational size of planets.

- Answering questions about the earth.

reaching the
STANDARDS with *RoundTable*

Standard 4

Life Sciences
Student understands the unity and diversity of life.

Teammates take turns:

- Listing anthropomorphic characteristics of a certain plant or animal.

- Recording the similarities of two plants or animals.

- Listing the things we do at different developmental stages of life (as a baby, as a kid, as a teenager, as an adult, or as an elder).

- Classifying animals as vertebrates or invertebrates.

- Reading about striking similarities among seemingly different animals.

Standard 5

Life Sciences
Student comprehends the basics of genetics.

Teammates take turns:

- Listing inheritable traits.

- Listing learned characteristics.

- Listing animals that are genetically similar to_____ and why. (Fill in any plant or animal.)

- Reading about the survival value of camouflage or listing animals and their unique camouflages.

- Listing the characteristics that are selectively advantageous to animals in a certain habitat (e.g., long necks for giraffes).

Standard 6

Life Sciences
Student knows the structure and function of cells and organisms.

Teammates take turns:

- Drawing the human skeleton, switching illustrators after each bone.

- Recording what they learned about the circulatory system.

- Diagramming steps of the digestive system.

- Measuring body parts and comparing them and their ratios (e.g., foot size: height) to those of teammates.

- Listing body structures and their functions.

reaching the
STANDARDS with *RoundTable*

Standard 7

Life Sciences
Student understands the interdependence of species and the environment.

Teammates take turns:

- Listing plants humans depend on and for what.

- Recording the effects _____ would have on animals or the environment (e.g., sharks become extinct, or oil tanker crashes).

- Listing the positive and negative effects humans have on the environment in a T-chart.

- Ranking the things that humans depend on to survive.

Standard 8

Life Sciences
Student understands the role of matter and energy in the environment.

Teammates take turns:

- Filling in details of a concept map on Energy in the Environment.

- Charting how energy can be transferred from one source to another in a rain forest.

- Listing sources of energy.

Standard 9

Life Sciences
Student comprehends the basics of the evolution of species.

Teammates take turns:

- Sequencing the appearance of various organisms on earth.

- Sequencing the disappearance of extinct animals.

- Making a contribution to a team project on evolution.

- Reading about the theory of evolution.

reaching the
STANDARDS with *RoundTable*

Standard 10

Physical Sciences
Student understands the basic properties of matter.

Teammates take turns:

• Weighing, measuring, and recording characteristics of a material.

• Generating descriptive words or phrases for the properties of a particular type of material.

• Listing ways to change the properties of a particular item (heating, freezing, dissolving, mixing, cutting, or bending).

• Listing the materials found in a car, where, and why (e.g., glass is used for the windshield because it is transparent and it protects the driver from bugs and dirt).

Standard 11

Physical Sciences
Student comprehends the types, sources, and conversions of energy and their relationship to heat and temperature.

Teammates take turns:

• Recording different ways they've seen one form of energy converted into another form in sports.

• Acting out different ways to keep warm.

• Listing things that run on electricity.

• Listing ways to conserve electricity.

• Writing how heat is created as a by-product of mechanical and electrical machines.

Standard 12

Physical Sciences
Student comprehends the principles of motion.

Teammates take turns:

• Filling in a T-chart with things that move fast and things that move slowly.

• Recording the sounds they hear in a noisy city and what motion produces the sounds.

• Listing actions and the reactions they produce.

• Demonstrating the various motions of an airplane using a model.

• Recording the motion of things they observe on the playground.

• Altering the motion of a swinging pendulum.

reaching the
STANDARDS with *RoundTable*

Standard 13	Standard 14	Standard 15
Physical Sciences	**Nature of Science**	**Nature of Science**
Student understands the forces between objects and within atoms.	*Student comprehends the nature of scientific knowledge.*	*Student comprehends the nature of scientific inquiry.*
Teammates take turns:	*Teammates take turns:*	*Teammates take turns:*
• Listing things that beat the force of gravity and describing how (e.g., a space shuttle overcomes gravity using force).	• Listing scientific findings that should be replicable.	• Rank ordering the most important tools to a scientist.
• Observing and recording things a magnet will stick to.	• Listing discoveries that happened long ago that are still important today.	• Sequencing the steps of the scientific method.
• Listing what might happen if there was no gravity.	• Matching up the scientist with his/her field of study (e.g., astronomer: studies the universe, stars, and planets).	• Generating additional questions their experiment produced.
		• Filling in what they know about a topic and what they would like to learn.

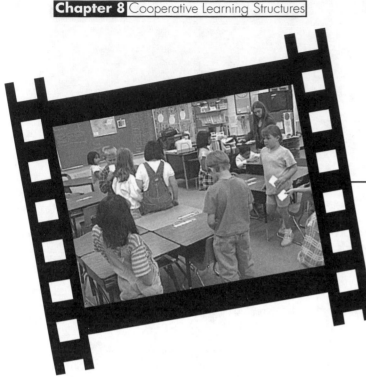

Mix-N-Match

With cards in hand, students "Mix" repeatedly in the classroom then search for their "Match," a student with a card that matches.

1 Students Mix

Each student is given a card relating to the content of study. Two cards make a match. For example, on one card there is the name or a picture of a cell part; on the second card, there is a description its function. With their cards in hand, students get out of their seats and mix in the classroom.

2 Partner A Asks

Students form pairs. Partner A asks a question based on his/her card: "I have the heart, what does the heart do?" Partner B answers.

3 Partner B Asks

Now, partner B asks a question based on his/her card: "I control the body's functioning and thinking. What am I?" Partner A answers.

4 Partners Trade Cards

Partners trade cards, pair up with a new partner, and ask each other questions based on their new cards. This is repeated until the teacher calls, "Freeze."

5 Teacher Calls Freeze

The teacher tells students to freeze. Students look at their new cards and think of the matching card. Teacher calls, "Make a match!"

6 Students Find Match

Students rush to the center of the room to look for their partner with the matching card. When they find their match, they move to the perimeter of the room. When all students are at the perimeter of the room, they have all found their match.

Management Tip

Make It Snappy

Mix-N-Match may be played for several rounds and a stopwatch may be used to record how long takes from the time the teacher calls, "Make a match!" until all students have found their partner. A class graph of times may be created and posted.

VIDEO in the

We see Laurie Kagan teaching teachers how to use Mix-N-Match. As students play Mix-N-Match they become familiar with the content and relations among the items. The content of Mix-N-Match can be any science content, whether students are matching animals with their names, compounds with their elements, or outcomes with the appropriate explanatory law of physics. This is a fun and engaging structure to master basic scientific knowledge.

Mix-N-Match

Mix-N-Match
ADAPTATIONS

Inclusion

Physical Disabilities
Some students will need help in moving around the room. If movement is not practical, classmates may need to come to the student.

Cognitive Disabilities
If the cards have questions that are significantly more advanced than the student is able to answer on his/her own, student may "twin" with a partner who can help explain. It is also possible to pre-teach questions and answers to increase success.

Behavioral or Emotional Disabilities
As long as the student is able to answer the questions and handle movement and proximity, this structure should not require accommodations.

ESL

Pre-Production
Pre-productive students each accompany a buddy who can model the necessary oral language.

Early Production to Intermediate Fluency
No adaptations necessary.

reaching the
STANDARDS with *Mix-N-Match*

Standard 1

Earth & Space Sciences
Student knows the basic features of Earth.

Classmates match up:

- Item with its composition (e.g., Tire ⇨ Rubber; Oak Desk ⇨ Wood).

- Matter with its state (e.g., Popsicle ⇨ Solid; Root beer ⇨ Liquid).

- Vocabulary word with its definition (e.g., Precipitation ⇨ Depositing rain, snow, sleet).

Standard 2

Earth & Space Sciences
Student understands the basic processes of Earth.

Classmates match up:

- Rock sample with a similar rock.

- Mineral sample with a card with the mineral's name.

- Natural disaster with its definition (e.g., Tornado ⇨ A violently whirling column of air with wind speeds of 160 to 480 km/hr).

- Natural disaster with a magazine picture of the effects of the natural disaster.

Standard 3

Earth & Space Sciences
Student comprehends Earth's place in the universe and the essential composition and structure of the universe.

Classmates match up:

- Planet names with planet picture cards.

- Planet name with their facts about the planet.

- Astronomer with their contribution.

- Celestial body or phenomenon with its definition (e.g., Comet ⇨ A small frozen mass of dust and gas revolving around the sun: as it nears the sun part of it vaporizes, forming a coma and usually a long tail that points away from the sun).

reaching the
STANDARDS with *Mix-N-Match*

Standard 4

Life Sciences
Student understands the unity and diversity of life.

Classmates match up:

- Animal name with its picture card.

- Plant with its picture card.

- Animal picture with its type of covering
(e.g., Bear ⇨ Fur;
Salmon ⇨ Scales;
Hawk ⇨ Feathers;
Human ⇨ Smooth skin).

- Animal picture with its category
(e.g., Dolphin ⇨ Mammal;
Cobra ⇨ Reptile;
Frog ⇨ Amphibian).

Standard 5

Life Sciences
Student comprehends the basics of genetics.

Classmates match up:

- Adult animal with its offspring
(e.g., Cat ⇨ Kitten;
Deer ⇨ Fawn;
Dog ⇨ Puppy).

- Seed with its fruit.

- Animal with animal in same phylum (e.g.,
Flatworm ⇨ Tapeworm;
Snail ⇨ Octopus;
Scorpion ⇨ Spider;
Starfish ⇨ Sea Urchin;
Human ⇨ Rabbit).

Standard 6

Life Sciences
Student knows the structure and function of cells and organisms.

Classmates match up:

- Bird picture card with its bill type (e.g., crushing, tearing, probing, skimming).

- Organ with its function (e.g.,
Heart ⇨ Pumping Blood;
Ear ⇨ Hearing;
Eye ⇨ Seeing;
Hand ⇨ Holding).

- Organ with its system (e.g.,
Brain ⇨ Nervous System;
Stomach ⇨ Digestive System).

- Part of a cell with picture or definition of cell part.

reaching the
STANDARDS with *Mix-N-Match*

Standard 7	Standard 8	Standard 9
Life Sciences	**Life Sciences**	**Life Sciences**
Student understands the interdependence of species and the environment.	*Student understands the role of matter and energy in the environment.*	*Student comprehends the basics of the evolution of species.*
Classmates match up:	*Classmates match up:*	*Classmates match up:*
• Animal with its home (e.g., Bird ⇨ Nest; Gopher ⇨ Tunnel; Beaver ⇨ Lodge; Human ⇨ House; Bat ⇨ Cave). • Animal with its natural habitat (e.g., Desert ⇨ Camel; Rain Forest ⇨ Toucan). • Animal with its order (e.g., Shark ⇨ Carnivore; Iguana ⇨ Herbivore; Human ⇨ Omnivore).	• Animal with its diet. • Predators with their prey.	• Present day animals with their ancestors. • Extinct animal with its name. • Endangered animal with its name.

reaching the
STANDARDS with *Mix-N-Match*

Standard 10

Physical Sciences
Student understands the basic properties of matter.

Classmates match up:

- Objects and their approximate weights.

- Object with its constituent parts (e.g., Bicycle ⇨ Two tires, rims, frame, handlebars, seat, pedals, chain, sprocket).

- Element with its atomic weight.

- Vocabulary word with its definition (magnetic, density, soluble, magnification).

Standard 11

Physical Sciences
Student comprehends the types, sources, and conversions of energy and their relationship to heat and temperature.

Classmates match up:

- Electrical terminology with definitions (alternating current, direct current, circuit, conductive, volts, amps, ohms, generator, battery, outlet, current).

- Energy terms with definitions (e.g., kinetic, potential, convection, radiation, conduction, insulation, temperature).

- Farenheit temperature with its Celsius equivalent.

Standard 12

Physical Sciences
Student comprehends the principles of motion.

Classmates match up:

- Object with the type of simple machine incorporated.

- Object in motion with direction of motion (e.g., Light ⇨ Straight Line; Sound ⇨ Waves; Merry-go-round ⇨ Circular).

- Object in motion with its top or approximate speed.

- Object in motion with type of force used to produce motion (thrust, friction, lift, tension).

- Vocabulary words and definitions (inertia, momentum, speed, acceleration, resistance).

reaching the
STANDARDS with *Mix-N-Match*

Standard 13

Physical Sciences
Student understands the forces between objects and within atoms.

Classmates match up:

- Newton's three laws of motion with examples.

- Picture cards of objects that a magnet will and will not stick to with cards that read "Yes" or "No."

- Force vocabulary cards with definitions (e.g., mass, gravity, magnetic, centrifugal, centripetal, inertia, weightlessness, mechanical force, subatomic force, attract, repel).

Standard 14

Nature of Science
Student comprehends the nature of scientific knowledge.

Classmates match up:

- Inventors with their inventions.

- Scientists with their discoveries.

- Scientists with their field of science.

- Field of science with definition.

Standard 15

Nature of Science
Student comprehends the nature of scientific inquiry.

Classmates match up:

- Scientific tools with their functions.

- Scientist with questions he or she might ask (e.g.: Astronomer ⇨ Is the earth the center of the universe?).

Resources

The Standards

Doyle, Denis P., & Susan Dimentel. *Raising the Standard, 2nd Edition.* Thousand Oaks, CA: Corwin Press, Inc., 1999. $29.95

Education Week (Publisher). *Quality Counts, 2000, Volume 19, Issue 18.* Washington, DC: 2000. $10.00

Foriska, Terry J. *Restructuring Around Standards: A Practitioner's Guide to Design and Implementation.* Thousand Oaks, CA: Corwin Press, Inc., 1998. $27.95

Kendall, John S., & Robert J. Marzano. *Content Knowledge: A Compendium of Standards & Benchmarks for K-12 Education, 2nd Edition.* Alexandria, VA: ASCD, 1997. $24.95

Kerzner-Lipsky, Dorothy, & Alan Gartner. *Standards & Inclusion: Can We Have Both? (Video).* Port Chester, NY: National Professional Resources, Inc., 1998. $99.00

Kohn, Alfie. *The Schools Our Children Deserve: Moving Beyond Traditional Classrooms and "Tougher Standards."* Boston, MA: Houghton Mifflin Company, 1999. $24.00

National Professional Resources, Inc. (Producer). *Service Learning: Curriculum, Standards and the Community (Video).* Port Chester, NY: 1998. $99.00

Rothman, Robert. *Measuring Up: Standards, Assessment, and School Reform.* San Francisco, CA: Jossey-Bass Publishers, 1995. $28.95

Schlechty, Phillip C. *Inventing Better Schools: An Action Plan for Educational Reform.* San Francisco, CA: Jossey-Bass Publishers, 1997. $27.00

Tucker, Marc S., & Judy B. Codding. *Standards for Our Schools: How to Set Them, Measure Them, and Reach Them.* San Francisco, CA: Jossey-Bass Publishers, 1998. $25.00

Organizations

AFT – American Federation of Teachers
555 New Jersey Ave, NW
Washington, DC 20001
www.aft.org

ASCD - Association for Supervision and Curriculum Development
1703 N. Beauregard Street
Alexandria, VA 22311-1714
(800) 933-2723
www.ascd.org

> For availability call,
> **National Professional Resources, Inc. • 1 (800) 453-7461**

Council for Basic Education
1319 F Street, NW
Suite 900
Washington, DC 20004-1152
(202) 347-4171
www.c-b-e.org

Education Commission of the States
707 17th Street
Suite 2700
Denver, CO 80202-3427
(303) 299-3600
www.ecs.org

McRel – Mid-Continent Regional Education Laboratory
2550 S. Parker Road
Suite 500
Aurora, CO 80014
(303) 337-0990
www.mcrel.org

NAESP – National Association of Elementary School Principals
1615 Duke Street
Alexandria, VA 22314
(800) 38-NAESP
www.naesp.org

NASSP – National Association of Secondary School Principals
1904 Association Drive
Reston, VA 20191-1537
(703) 860-0200
www.nassp.org

National Board for Professional Teaching Standards
26555 Evergreen Road
Suite 400
Southfield, MD 48076
(800) 229-9074
www.nbpts.org

National Professional Resources, Inc.
25 South Regent Street
Port Chester, NY 10573
(800) 453-7461
www.nprinc.com

NEA – National Education Association
1201 16th Street NW
Washington, DC 20036
(202) 833-4000
www.nea.org

New American Schools
1560 Wilson Blvd.
Suite 901
Arlington, VA 22209
(703) 908-9500
www.naschools.org

OERI – Office of Educational Research and Improvement
US Department of Education
Washington, DC 20208-5570
(202) 205-9864
www.ed.gov

United Federation of Teachers
260 Park Avenue South
New York, NY 10010
(212) 777-7500
www.uft.org

US Office of Education
Washington, DC 20202
(202) 205-9864
www.ed.gov

Cooperative Learning

Kagan, Laurie, Miguel, & Spencer. *Cooperative Learning Structures for Teambuilding.* San Clemente, CA: Kagan Publishing, 1997. $25.00

Kagan, Miguel & Spencer, & Laurie Robertson. *Cooperative Learning Structures for Classbuilding.* San Clemente, CA: Kagan Publishing, 1995. $25.00

Kagan, Spencer. *Cooperative Learning.* San Clemente, CA: Kagan Publishing, 1994. $35.00

Kagan, Spencer. *Building Character Through Cooperative Learning (Video).* Port Chester, NY: National Professional Resources, Inc., 1999. $99.95

Putnam, JoAnne W. *Cooperative Learning and Strategies for Inclusion.* Baltimore, MD: Paul H. Brookes Publishing, 1998. $26.95

Rimmerman, Harlan (Editor). *Resources in Cooperative Learning.* San Clemente, CA: Kagan Cooperative Learning, 1996. $18.75

Organizations

ASCD Cooperative Learning Network
Contact: Debra Smith
Rockhurst College
1100 Rockhurst Road
Kansas City, MO 64110-2561
(816) 501-4148

Cooperative Learning Center
Contact: Roger Johnson, Chair
University of Minnesota
202 Pattee Hall
150 Pillsbury Drive, DE
Minneapolis, MN 55455
(612) 624-7031

For availability call,
National Professional Resources, Inc. • 1 (800) 453-7461

Kagan Publishing & Professional Development
1160 Calle Cordillera
San Clemente, CA 92673
(800) 933-2667
www.KaganOnline.com

National Professional Resources, Inc.
25 South Regent Street
Port Chester, NY 10573
(800) 453-7461
www.nprinc.com

Inclusion/ Special Education

Anderson, Winifred, Stephen Chitwood, & Diedre Hayden. *Negotiating the Special Education Maze.* Bethesda, MD: Woodbine House, 1997. $16.95

Armstrong, Thomas. *The Myth of the A.D.D. Child.* New York, NY: Penguin Putnam Inc., 1997. $13.95

Batshaw, Mark L. *Children with Disabilities, 4th Edition.* Baltimore, MD: Paul H. Brookes Publishing, 1997. $33.95

Block, Martin E. *A Teacher's Guide to Including Students With Disabilities in Regular Physical Education.* Baltimore, MD: Paul H. Brookes Publishing, 1994. $39.00

Buehler, Bruce. *What We Know...How We Teach – Linking Medicine & Education for the Child with Special Needs (Video).* Port Chester, NY: National Professional Resources, Inc., 1998. $99.95

Bunch, Gary. *Inclusion: How To.* Toronto, Canada: Inclusion Press, 1999. $19.95

Dover, Wendy. *The Inclusion Facilitator (three-ring binder).* Manhattan, KS: MASTER Teacher, 1994. $49.95

Dover, Wendy. *The Personal Planner & Training Guide for the Para Professional (three-ring binder).* Manhattan, KS: MASTER Teacher, 1996. $19.95

Dover, Wendy. *Inclusion: The Next Step (three-ring binder).* Manhattan, KS: MASTER Teacher, 1999. $44.95

Downing, June E. *Including Students with Severe and Multiple Disabilities in Typical Classrooms.* Baltimore, MD: Paul H. Brookes Publishing, 1996. $32.95

For availability call,
National Professional Resources, Inc. • 1 (800) 453-7461

Falvey, Mary A. *Inclusive and Heterogeneous Schooling: Assessment, Curriculum, and Instruction.* Baltimore, MD: Paul H Brookes Publishing, 1995. $34.95

Fisher, Douglas, Caren Sax, & Ian Pumpian. *Inclusive High Schools.* Baltimore, MD: Paul H. Brookes Publishing, 1999. $26.00

Flick, Grad L. *ADD/ADHD Behavior-Change Resource Kit.* West Nyack, NY: Center for Applied Research in Education, 1998. $29.95

Forum on Education (Producer). *Adapting Curriculum & Instruction in Inclusive Classrooms (Video).* Bloomington, IN: 1999. $129.95

Giangreco, Michael F. *Quick-Guides to Inclusion: Ideas for Educating Students with Disabilities.* Baltimore, MD: Paul H. Brookes Publishing, 1997. $21.95

Giangreco, Michael F. *Quick-Guides to Inclusion 2.* Baltimore, MD: Paul H. Brookes Publishing, 1998. $21.95

Giangreco, Michael, Chigee J. Cloninger, & Virginia Salce Iverson. *Choosing Outcomes & Accommodations for Children (COACH), 2nd Edition.* Baltimore, MD: Paul H. Brookes Publishing, 1998. $37.95

Glasser, William. *Alternative Strategies to Social Promotion (Video).* Port Chester, NY: National Professional Resources, Inc., 1998. $99.95

Goodman, Gretchen. *Inclusive Classrooms from A to Z: A Handbook for Educators.* Columbus, OH: Teachers' Publishing Group, 1996. $26.95

Guilford Press (Producer). *Assessing ADHD in the Schools (Video).* New York, NY: 1999. $99.95

Guilford Press (Producer). *Classroom Interventions for ADHD (Video).* New York, NY: 1999. $99.95

Hammeken, Peggy A. *Inclusion: An Essential Guide for the Para Professional.* Minnetonka, MN: Peytral Publications, 1996. $21.95

Hammeken, Peggy A. *Inclusion: 450 Strategies for Success.* Minnetonka, MN: Peytral Publications, 1997. $21.95

Harry, Beth. *Cultural Diversity, Families, and the Special Education System.* New York, NY: Teachers College Press, 1992. $22.95

Harwell, Joan M. *Ready-to-Use Information & Materials for Assessing Specific Learning Disabilities, Volume I.* West Nyack, NY: Center for Applied Research in Education, 1995. $27.95

For availability call,
National Professional Resources, Inc. • 1 (800) 453-7461

Harwell, Joan M. *Ready-to-Use Tools & Materials for Remediating Specific Learning Disabilities, Volume II.* West Nyack, NY: Center for Applied Research in Education, 1995. $27.95

Harwell, Joan M. *Ready-to-Use Learning Disability Activities Kit.* West Nyack, NY: Center for Applied Research in Education, 1993. $27.95

HBO (Producer). *Educating Peter (Video).* New York, NY: 1993. $79.95

Jorgensen, Cheryl M. *Restructuring High Schools for All Students.* Baltimore, MD: Paul H. Brookes Publishing, 1998. $27.95

Kagan, Spencer, & Laurie. *Reaching Standards Through Cooperative Learning: Providing for ALL Learners in General Education Classrooms (4-video series).* Port Chester, NY: National Professional Resources, Inc., 1999. $499.00

Kame'enui, Edward J., & Deborah C. Simmons. *Adapting Curricular Materials, Volume 1: An Overview of Materials Adaptations – Toward Successful Inclusion of Students with Disabilities: The Architecture of Instruction.* Reston, VA: Council for Exceptional Children, 1999. $11.40

Keefe, Charlotte Hendrick. *Label-Free Learning: Supporting Learners with Disabilities.* York, ME: Stenhouse Publishers, 1996. $19.50

Kennedy, Eileen. *Ready-to-Use Lessons & Activities for the Inclusive Primary Classroom.* West Nyack, NY: Center for Applied Research in Education, 1997. $28.95

Kerzner-Lipsky, Dorothy, & Alan Gartner. *Inclusion and School Reform.* Baltimore, MD: Paul H. Brookes Publishing, 1997. $36.95

Kerzner-Lipsky, Dorothy, & Alan Gartner. *Standards & Inclusion: Can We Have Both? (Video).* Port Chester, NY: National Professional Resources, Inc., 1998. $99.00

Kliewer, Christopher. *Schooling Children with Down Syndrome.* New York, NY: Teachers College Press, 1998. $21.95

Lang, Greg, & Chirs Berberich. *All Children Are Special: Creating an Inclusive Classroom.* York, ME: Stenhouse Publishers, 1995. $19.50

MASTER Teacher (Producer). *Lesson Plans & Modifications for Inclusion and Collaborative Classrooms (4-video series).* Manhattan, KS: 1995. $498.00

For availability call,
National Professional Resources, Inc. • 1 (800) 453-7461

MASTER Teacher (Producer). *Inclusion: The Next Step (4-video series).* Manhattan, KS: 1999. $498.00

MASTER Teacher (Producer). *Inclusion Video Series (4-video series).* Manhattan, KS: 1994. $498.00

MASTER Teacher (Publisher). *Lesson Plans and Modifications for Inclusion and Collaborative Classrooms (three-ring binder).* Manhattan, KS: 1995. $59.95

MASTER Teacher (Publisher). *Lesson Plans and Modifications for Inclusion and Collaborative Classrooms, Book 2 (three-ring binder).* Manhattan, KS: 1996. $59.95

Meyen, Edward L., Glenn A. Vergason, & Richard J. Whelan. *Strategies for Teaching Exceptional Children in Inclusive Settings.* Denver, CO: Love Publishing, 1996. $45.00

Moore, Lorraine O. *Inclusion: Strategies for Working with Young Children.* Minnetonka, MN: Peytral Publications, 1997. $19.95

Pierangelo, Roger, & Rochelle Crane. *Complete Guide to Special Education Transition Services.* West Nyack, NY: Center for Applied Research in Education, 1997. $29.95

Pierangelo, Roger. *The Special Education Teacher's Book of Lists.* West Nyack, NY: Center for Applied Research in Education, 1995. $29.95

Porter, Stephanie, et al. *Children and Youth – Assisted by Medical Technology in Educational Settings: Guidelines for Care.* Baltimore, MD: Paul H. Brookes Publishing, 1997. $52.00

Putnam, JoAnne W. *Cooperative Learning and Strategies for Inclusion.* Baltimore, MD: Paul H. Brookes Publishing, 1998. $26.95

Rief, Sandra F. *The ADD/ADHD Checklist.* Paramus, NJ: Prentice Hall, 1998. $11.95

Rief, Sandra F. *How to Reach and Teach ADD/ADHD Children.* West Nyack, NY: Center for Applied Research in Education, 1993. $27.95

Rief, Sandra F., & Julie A. Heimburge. *How to Reach & Teach All Students in the Inclusive Classroom.* West Nyack, NY: Center for Applied Research in Education, 1996. $28.50

Rief, Sandra. *ADHD – Inclusive Instruction & Collaborative Practices (Video).* Port Chester, NY: National Professional Resources, Inc., 1995. $99.00

For availability call,
National Professional Resources, Inc. • 1 (800) 453-7461

Rief, Sandra. *How to Help Your Child Succeed in School: Strategies and Guidance for Parents of Children with ADHD and/or Learning Disabilities (Video).* Port Chester, NY: National Professional Resources, Inc., 1997. $46.00

Sage, Daniel D. *Inclusion in Secondary Schools.* Port Chester, NY: National Professional Resources, Inc., 1997. $29.95

Sapon-Shevin, Mara. *Because We Can Change the World.* Boston, MA: Allyn & Bacon, 1999. $29.95

Schumaker, Jean, & Keith Lenz. *Adapting Curricular Materials, Volume 3: Grades Six Through Eight – Adapting Language Arts, Social Studies, and Science Materials for the Inclusive Classroom.* Reston, VA: Council for Exceptional Children, 1999. $11.40

Shum, Jeanne Shay. *Adapting Curricular Materials, Volume 2: Kindergarten Through Grade Five – Adapting Reading & Math Materials for the Inclusive Classroom.* Reston, VA: Council for Exceptional Children, 1999. $11.40

Stainback, Susan, & William. *Inclusion: A Guide for Educators.* Baltimore, MD: Paul H. Brookes Publishing, 1996. $33.95

Strichart, Stephen S., Charles T. Mangrum II, & Patricia Iannuzzi. *Teaching Study Skills and Strategies to Students with Learning Disabilities, Attention Deficit Disorders, or Special Needs, 2nd Edition.* Boston, MA: Allyn & Bacon, 1998. $29.95

Thousand, Jacqueline S., Richard A. Villa, & Ann I. Nevin. *Creating Collaborative Learning: A Practical Guide to Empowering Students & Teachers.* Baltimore, MD: Paul H. Brookes Publishing, 1994. $37.00

Thurlow, Martha L., Judy L. Elliott, & James E. Ysseldyke. *Testing Students with Disabilities.* Thousand Oaks, CA: Corwin Press, 1998. $29.95

U.S. Department of Education (Publisher). *To Assure the Free Appropriate Public Education of All Children with Disabilities.* Washington, DC: 1998. Free

VanDover, Theresa. *A Principal's Guide to Creating a Building Climate for Inclusion (3-ring binder).* Manhattan, KS: MASTER Teacher, 1995. $44.95

Villa, Richard A., & Jacqueline S. Thousand. *Restructuring for Caring and Effective Education.* Baltimore, MD: Paul H. Brookes Publishing, 2000. $44.95

For availability call,
National Professional Resources, Inc. • 1 (800) 453-7461

Winebrenner, Susan. *Teaching Kids with Learning Difficulties in the Regular Classroom.* Minneapolis, MN: Free Spirit Publishing, 1996. $27.95

Organizations

CHADD – Children and Adults with Attention Deficit Disorders
8181 Professional Place
Suite 201
Landover, MD 20875
(301) 306-7070 or (800) 233-4050
www.chadd.org

ERIC – Educational Resources Information Center Clearinghouse on Disabilities and Gifted Education CEC - The Council for Exceptional Children
1920 Association Drive
Reston, VA 20191-1589
(800) 328-0272

Exceptional Parent
555 Kinderkamack Road
Oradell, NJ 07649-1517
(201) 634-6550
www.eparent.com

KDWB Variety Family Center University of Minnesota Gateway
200 Oak Street SE
Suite 160
Minneapolis, MN 55455
(612) 626-2401
www.peds.umn.edu/peds-adol

National Association of State Directors of Special Education, Inc.
1800 Diagonal Road
Suite 320
Alexandria, VA 22314
(703) 519-3800
www.nasdse.org

National Professional Resources, Inc.
25 South Regent Street
Port Chester, NY 10573
(800) 453-7461
www.nprinc.com

NICHCY – National Information Center for Children and Youth with Disabilities
P O Box 1492
Washington, DC 20013-1492
(800) 695-0285
www.nichcy.org

NPND – The National Parent Network on Disabilities
1130 17th Street, NW
Suite 400
Washington, DC 20036
(202) 463-9405
www.npnd.org

OSEP – Office of Special Education Programs US Department of Education
Washington, DC 20202
www.ed.gov/OFFICES/OSERS/OSEP/index.html

**OSERS – US Department of Education
The Office of Special Education and Rehabilitative Services**
600 Independence Avenue, SW
Washington, DC 20202
(202) 205-9864
www.ed.gov/OFFICES/OSERS

English As a Second Language (ESL)

Cary, Stephen. *Second Language Learners.* York, ME: Stenhouse Publishers, 1997. $18.75

Claire, Elizabeth. *ESL Teacher's Activities Kit.* Englewood Cliffs, NJ: Prentice Hall, 1998. $29.50

Delpit, Lisa. *Other People's Children: Cultural Conflict in the Classroom.* New York, NY: The New Press, 1995. $14.95

Gonzalez, Maria Luisa, Anna Huerta-Macias, & Josefina Villamil Tinajero (Editors). *Educating Latino Students.* Lancaster, PA: Technomic Publishing, 1998. $44.95

Grevious, Saundrah Clark. *Ready-to-Use Multicultural Activities for Primary Children.* West Nyack, NY: Center for Applied Research in Education, 1993. $27.95

Gusman, Jo. *Multiple Intelligences and the 2nd Language Learner (Video).* Port Chester, NY: National Professional Resources, Inc., 1998. $99.95

High, Julie. *Second Language Learning Through Cooperative Learning.* San Clemente, CA: Kagan Cooperative Learning, 1993. $25.00

Koss-Chioino, Joan D., & Luis A. Vargas. *Working with Latino Youth.* San Francisco, CA: Jossey-Bass, 1999. $34.95

Kress, Jacqueline E. *The ESL Teacher's Book of Lists.* Englewood Cliffs, NJ: Prentice Hall, 1998. $29.50

Manning, M. Lee, & Leroy G. Baruth. *Multicultural Education of Children and Adolescents.* Boston, MA: Allyn & Bacon, 1996. $39.95

For availability call,
National Professional Resources, Inc. • 1 (800) 453-7461

MASTER Teacher (Producer). *English as a Second Language (4-video series).* Manhattan, KS: 1998. $498.00

Miramontes, Ofelia B., Adel Nadeau, & Nancy L. Commins. *Restructuring Schools for Linguistic Diversity.* New York, NY: Teachers College Press, 1997. $23.95

Richard-Amato, Patricia A., & Marguerite Ann Snow. *The Multicultural Classroom.* Reading, MA: Addison-Wesley Publishing, 1992. $35.95

Rong, Xue Lan, & Judith Preissle. *Educating Immigrant Students.* Thousand Oaks, CA: Corwin Press, 1998. $24.95

Organizations

ACTFL – American Council on the Teaching of Foreign Languages
6 Executive Plaza
Yonkers, NY 10701-6801
(914) 963-8830
www.actfl.org

Institute of International Education
809 United Nations Plaza
New York, NY 10017-3580
(212) 883-8200
www.iie.org

Linguistic Society of America
1325 18th Street, NW
Suite 211
Washington, DC 20036-6501
(202) 835-1714
www.lsadc.org

NABE – National Association for Bilingual Education
Suite 605
1220 L Street, NW
Washington, DC 20005-4018
(202) 898-1829
www.nabe.org

National Professional Resources, Inc.
25 South Regent Street
Port Chester, NY 10573
(800) 453-7461
www.nprinc.com

TESOL – Teachers of English to Speakers of Other Languages, Inc.
700 S. Washington Street
Suite 200
Alexandria, VA 22314
(703) 836-0774
www.tesol.edu

For availability call,
National Professional Resources, Inc. • 1 (800) 453-7461

Multiple Intelligences & Emotional Intelligence

Armstrong, Thomas. *Multiple Intelligences: Discovering the Giftedness in ALL (Video).* Port Chester, NY: National Professional Resources, Inc., 1997. $79.00

Armstrong, Thomas. *7 Kinds of Smart: Identifying and Developing Your Many Intelligences.* New York, NY: Penguin Group, 1993. $12.95

Berman, Sally. *Service Learning for the Multiple Intelligences Classroom.* Arlington Heights, IL: Skylight Training and Publishing Inc., 1999. $34.95

Bocchino, Rob. *Emotional Literacy: To Be a Different Kind of Smart.* Thousand Oaks, CA: Corwin Press, 1999. $24.95

Bruetsch, Ann. *Multiple Intelligences Lesson Plan Book.* Tucson, AZ: Zephyr Press, 1995. $35.00

Buggeman, Sally, Tom Hoerr, & Christine Wallach (Editors). *Celebrating Multiple Intelligences: Teaching for Success.* St. Louis, MO: The New City School, Inc., 1994. $24.95

Buggeman, Sally, Tom Hoerr, & Christine Wallach (Editors). *Succeeding with Multiple Intelligences: Teaching Through the Personal Intelligences.* St. Louis, MO: The New City School, Inc., 1996. 1996. $34.00

Campbell, Bruce. *The Multiple Intelligences Handbook.* Stanwood, WA: Campbell & Associates, Inc., 1994. $25.00

Campbell, Linda & Bruce, & Dee Dickinson. *Teaching and Learning Through Multiple Intelligences, 2nd Edition.* Boston, MA: Allyn & Bacon, 1999. $32.95

Carreiro, Paul. *Tales of Thinking: Multiple Intelligences in the Classroom.* York, ME: Stenhouse Publishers, 1998. $16.00

Cohen, Jonathan. *Educating Minds and Hearts: Social Emotional Learning and the Passage into Adolescence.* New York, NY: Teachers College Press, 1999. $21.95

For availability call,
National Professional Resources, Inc. • 1 (800) 453-7461

Freedman, Joshua M., Anabel L. Jensen, Marsha C. Rideout, & Patricia E. Freedman. *Handle with Care: Emotional Intelligence Activity Book.* San Mateo, CA: Six Seconds, 1998. $16.95

Gardner, Howard. *Frames of Mind: The Theory of Multiple Intelligences.* New York, NY: Basic Books, 1983.

Gardner, Howard. *Intelligence Reframed: Multiple Intelligences for the 21st Century.* New York, NY: Basic Books, 1999. $27.50

Gardner, Howard. *Multiple Intelligences: The Theory in Practice.* New York, NY: Basic Books, 1993. $18.50

Gardner, Howard. *The Disciplined Mind: What All Students Should Understand.* New York, NY: Simon & Schuster, 1999. $25.00

Gardner, Howard. *How Are Kids Smart? Multiple Intelligences in the Classroom, Teacher's Version (Video).* Port Chester, NY: National Professional Resources, Inc., 1995. $69.00

Gardner, Howard. *Multiple Intelligences: Intelligence, Understanding and the Mind (2-video set with teaching guide).* Los Angeles, CA: Into the Classroom Media, 1999. $199.00

Goleman, Daniel. *Emotional Intelligence: Why It Can Matter More Than IQ.* New York, NY: Bantam Books, 1995. $13.95

Goleman, Daniel. *Emotional Intelligence: A New Vision for Educators (Video).* Port Chester, NY: National Professional Resources, Inc., 1996. $89.95

Griffith, Sally Cardoza. *Multiple Intelligences: Teaching Kids the Way They Learn (Grade 1).* Torrance, CA: Frank Schaffer Publications, Inc., 1999. $9.95

Gusman, Jo. *Multiple Intelligences and the Second Language Learner (Video).* Port Chester, NY: National Professional Resources, Inc., 1998. $46.00

Hall, M.C. *Multiple Intelligences: Teaching Kids the Way They Learn (Grade 4).* Torrance, CA: Frank Schaffer Publications, Inc., 1999. $9.95

Hoffman, Barbara G., & Kim Thuman. *Multiple Intelligences: Teaching Kids the Way They Learn (Grade 3).* Torrance, CA: Frank Schaffer Publications, Inc., 1999. $9.95

Kagan, Spencer, & Miguel. *Multiple Intelligences: The Complete MI Book.* San Clemente, CA: Kagan Publishing, 1998. $39.95

For availability call,
National Professional Resources, Inc. • 1 (800) 453-7461

Lazear, David. *Multiple Intelligence Approaches to Assessment: Solving the Assessment Conundrum.* Tucson, AZ: Zephyr Press, 1994. $39.00

Lazear, David. *Seven Pathways of Learning: Teaching Students and Parents About Multiple Intelligences.* Tucson, AZ: Zephyr Press, 1994. $35.00

LeDoux, Joseph. *The Emotional Brain: The Mysterious Underpinnings of Emotional Life.* New York, NY: Touchstone, 1996. $14.00

MASTER Teacher (Publisher). *Lesson Plans: For Incorporating Multiple Intelligences Into the Curriculum and the Classroom, Elementary Edition.* Manhattan, KS: 1999. $49.95

Prior, Jennifer Overend. *Multiple Intelligences: Teaching Kids the Way They Learn (Grade 5).* Torrance, CA: Frank Schaffer Publications, Inc., 1999. $9.95

Salovey, Peter, & David J. Sluyter (Editors). *Emotional Development and Emotional Intelligence.* New York, NY: Basic Books, 1997. $44.00

Steele, Ann L. *Multiple Intelligences: Teaching Kids the Way They Learn (Grade 2).* Torrance, CA: Frank Schaffer Publications, Inc., 1999. $9.95

Teele, Sue. *Rainbows of Intelligence: Exploring How Students Learn.* Redlands, CA: Sue Teele, 1999. $29.95

Teele, Sue. *The Multiple Intelligences School: A Place for All Students to Succeed.* Redlands, CA: Sue Teele, 1995. $25.00

Teele, Sue. *Rainbows of Intelligence: Raising Student Performance Through Multiple Intelligences (Video).* Port Chester, NY: National Professional Resources, Inc., 2000. $99.95

Wahl, Mark. *Math for Humans: Teaching Math Through 8 Intelligences, Revised Edition.* Langley, Washington: LivnLern Press, 1999. $29.95

Waldman, Naomi J. *Multiple Intelligences: Teaching Kids the Way They Learn (Grade 6).* Torrance, CA: Frank Schaffer Publications, Inc., 1999. $9.95

Organizations

ASCD – Association for Supervision and Curriculum Development
1703 N. Beauregard Street
Alexandria, VA 22311-1714
(800) 933-2723
www.ascd.org

For availability call,
National Professional Resources, Inc. • 1 (800) 453-7461

CASEL – Collaborative to Advance Social and Emotional Learning
University of Illinois at Chicago
Department of Psychology
1008 West Harrison Street
Chicago, IL 60607-7137
(312) 413-1008
www.casel.org

Center for Educational Outreach and Innovation Teachers College, Columbia University
300 Central Park West
New York, NY 10024-1513
(212) 877-7328
www.tc.columbia.edu/~academic/csel

Harvard Project Zero
321 Longfellow Hall
13 Appian Way
Cambridge, MA 02138
(617) 495-4342
www.pzweb.harvard.edu

National Professional Resources, Inc.
25 South Regent Street
Port Chester, NY 10573
(800) 453-7461
www.nprinc.com

Additional Resources

Allington, Richard L. & Patricia M. Cunningham. *Schools That Work: Where All Children Read and Write.* New York: NY, Harper Collins, 1996. $26.00

Beecher, Margaret. *Developing the Gifts & Talents of All Students in the Regular Classroom.* Mansfield Center, T: Creative Learning Press, Inc., 1995. $42.95

Darling-Hammond, Linda. *The New Teacher: Meeting the Challenges (Video).* Port Chester, NY: National Professional Resources, Inc., 2000. $99.95

Darling-Hammond, Linda. *The Right to Learn: A Blueprint for Creating Schools That Work.* San Francisco, CA: Jossey-Bass Publishers, 1997. $27.00

Darling-Hammond, Linda, Jacqueline Ancess, & Beverly Falk. *Authentic Assessment in Action: Studies of Schools and Students at Work.* New York, NY: Teachers College Press, 1995. $24.95

For availability call,
National Professional Resources, Inc. • 1 (800) 453-7461

Gardner, Howard, Daniel Goleman, Mihaly Csikszentmihalyi, & Peter Salovey. *Optimizing Intelligences: Thinking, Emotion & Creativity (Video).* Port Chester, NY: National Professional Resources Inc., 1999. $99.95

Glasser, William. *Building a Quality School: A Matter of Responsibility, Revised (Video).* Port Chester, NY: National Professional Resources, Inc., 1998. $99.00

Kagan, Spencer, & Laurie. *Reaching Standards Through Cooperative Learning: Providing for ALL Learners in General Education Classrooms (4-video series).* Port Chester, NY: National Professional Resources, Inc., 1999. $499.00

Miller, Wilma H. *Alternative Assessment Techniques for Reading & Writing.* West Nyack, NY: Center for Applied Research in Education, 1995. $29.95

Pert, Candace B. *Emotion: Gatekeeper to Performance – The Mind/Body Connection (Video).* Port Chester, NY: National Professional Resources, Inc., 1999. $99.00

Purcell, Jeanne H., & Joseph S. Renzulli. *Total Talent Portfolio: A Systematic Plan to Identify and Nurture Gifts and Talents.* Mansfield Center, CT: Creative Learning Press, Inc., 1998. $19.95

Reis, Sally M., Deborah E. Burns, & Joseph S. Renzulli. *Curriculum Compacting: The Complete Guide to Modifying the Regular Curriculum for High Ability Students.* Mansfield Center, CT: Creative Learning Press, Inc., 1992. $24.95

Renzulli, Joseph S. *Developing the Gifts and Talents of ALL Students: The Schoolwide Enrichment Model (Video).* Port Chester, NY: National Professional Resources, 1999. $99.95

Renzulli, Joseph S., & Sally M. Reis. *The Schoolwide Enrichment Model: A How-To Guide for Educational Excellence.* Mansfield Center, CT: Creative Learning Press, Inc., 1997. $42.95

Wiggins, Grant. *Educative Assessment: Designing Assessments to Inform and Improve Student Performance.* San Francisco, CA: Jossey-Bass Publishers, 1998. $34.95

For availability call,
National Professional Resources, Inc. • 1 (800) 453-7461

Science

Burz, Helen L., & Kit Marshall. *Performance-Based Curriculum for Science: From Knowing to Showing.* Thousand Oaks, CA: Corwin Press, 1997. $24.95

Candler, Laura. *Cooperative Learning & Hands-On Science.* San Clemente, CA: Kagan Publishing, 1995. $25.00

Candler, Laura. *Cooperative Learning & Wee Science.* San Clemente, CA: Kagan Publishing, 1995. $25.00

Candler, Laura. *Science Buddies. Cooperative Send-Home Science.* San Clemente, CA: Kagan Publishing, 1996. $15.00

DeBolt, Virginia. *Write! Science. Multiple Intelligences & Cooperative Learning Writing Activities.* San Clemente, CA: Kagan Publishing, 1996. $20.00

Educational Resources Information Center (Publisher). *The ERIC Review: K–8 Science and Mathematics Education, Volume 6, Issue 2.* Washington, DC: 1999. Free

Glock, Jenna, Susan Wertz, & Maggie Meyer. *Discovering the Naturalist Intelligence: Science in the School Yard.* Tucson, AZ: Zephyr Press, 1999. $29.00

Kagan, Miguel. *Higher-Level Thinking Questions for Life and Earth Sciences.* San Clemente, CA: Kagan Publishing, 1999. $19.00

Kagan, Miguel. *Higher-Level Thinking Questions for Physical Sciences.* San Clemente, CA: Kagan Publishing, 1999. $19.00

Kendall, John S., & Robert J. Marzano. *Content Knowledge: A Compendium of Standards & Benchmarks for K-12 Education, 2nd Edition.* Alexandria, VA: ASCD, 1997. $24.95

National Research Council (Editor). *National Science Education Standards.* Washington, DC: National Academy Press, 1996. $19.95

Rakow, Steven J. (Editor). *NSTA Pathways to the Science Standards.* Arlington, VA: National Science Teachers Association, 1998. $29.95

Samuels, Linda S. *Girls Can Succeed in Science! Antidotes for Science Phobia in Boys and Girls.* Thousand Oaks, CA: Corwin Press, 1999. $29.95

For availability call,
National Professional Resources, Inc. • 1 (800) 453-7461

Tolman, Marvin N. *Hands-On Science Activities for Grades K–2.* West Nyack, NY: Parker Publishing Co., 1999. $28.95

Tolman, Marvin N. *Hands-On Science Activities for Grades 3–4.* West Nyack, NY: Parker Publishing Co., 1999. $28.95

Tolman, Marvin N. *Hands-On Science Activities for Grades 5-6.* West Nyack, NY: Parker Publishing Co., 1999. $28.95

Organizations

AAAS - American Association for the Advancement of Science
1333 H Street, NW
Washington, DC 20005
(202) 326-6400

ERIC – Educational Resources Information Center Science, Mathematics, and Environmental Education
The Ohio State University
1929 Kenny Road
Columbus, OH 43210-1080
(800) 276-0462
www.ericse.org

National Research Council National Academy of Science
2101 Constitution Avenue, NW
Washington, DC 20418
(202) 334-2000
www.nationalacademies.org

NSTA - National Science Teachers Association
1840 Wilson Boulevard
Arlington, VA 22201-3000
(703) 243-7100
www.nsta.org